Leap of Faith

Transforming Physical and Emotional
Pain into Spiritual Growth

Jeffrey D. Millman, M.D.

BALBOA.
PRESS
A DIVISION OF HAY HOUSE

Balboa Press books may be ordered through booksellers or by contacting:

Balboa Press
A Division of Hay House
1663 Liberty Drive
Bloomington, IN 47403
www.balboapress.com
1-(877) 407-4847

Because of the dynamic nature of the Internet, any web addresses or links contained in this book may have changed since publication and may no longer be valid. The views expressed in this work are solely those of the author and do not necessarily reflect the views of the publisher, and the publisher hereby disclaims any responsibility for them.

ISBN: 978-1-4525-4705-3 (sc)
ISBN: 978-1-4525-4707-7 (hc)
ISBN: 978-1-4525-4706-0 (e)
Library of Congress Control Number: 2012903029

The author of this book does not dispense medical advice or prescribe the use of any technique as a form of treatment for physical, emotional, or medical problems without the advice of a physician, either directly or indirectly. The intent of the author is only to offer information of a general nature to help you in your quest for emotional and spiritual well-being. In the event you use any of the information in this book for yourself, which is your constitutional right, the author and the publisher assume no responsibility for your actions.

Any people depicted in stock imagery provided by Thinkstock are models, and such images are being used for illustrative purposes only.
Certain stock imagery © Thinkstock.

Printed in the United States of America

Balboa Press rev. date: 3/19/2012

I dedicate this book to my most important teacher

Patty

I wish to sincerely thank

Tara Millman-Martin

for transcribing this book

and

for her unfailing emotional support

Table of Contents

Introduction

This book is about your pain. It's about making sense of the problems you face every day. Illness, accidents, aging, relationship issues, worrying, depression, natural disasters—take your pick: at one time or another you will be challenged by each of life's difficulties.

You may feel victimized by the people or circumstances in your life, overwhelmed, and fearful. Sometimes you get angry at others or yourself, wanting to blame someone, anyone, for your situation. Most of the time you simply endure your lot in life, at times wondering if there's a reason for your suffering. Yet you lack answers and simply carry on day by day.

Medical science has identified some of the reasons we experience illness. Genetics predispose us to certain diseases. Lifestyle choices—nutrition, exercise, use of tobacco and alcohol—affect our health. Stress is a major factor in suppressing our immune system's ability to protect us from illness.

There is yet another component to understanding illness or emotional pain: spirituality. In my practice of medicine I approach healing from a holistic perspective: heart, mind, body, and spirit. Each of these aspects of being human affects the others. There is a constant interplay among our emotions, our thoughts, and the physiological functioning of the various organs in the body. What is often overlooked is the effect spirit has on how our life unfolds. Many of the explanations for your pain involve the spiritual component of the human experience.

Your soul, your Higher self, existed before you were born. It entered your physical body to give you life, and by virtue of this life provide you with life experiences, all of which are opportunities to learn the lessons you need to learn. All of us have our own particular sets of lessons to learn, so each of our lives is different in its details. Some of your life experiences are fun and you take pleasure in them. But it is the painful ones that force you to face the various issues required for your soul to grow. All living things grow. Your soul inherently seeks growth in its desire for enlightenment. To achieve oneness with your Higher Power your soul must overcome such issues as anger, fear, greed, jealousy, and self-loathing. Over the course of many lifetimes you will eventually deal successfully with them all.

Understanding the meaning behind human suffering requires you to use your full brain—both your rational mind and your intuitive mind. The rational mind uses the five senses—sight, smell, hearing, taste, and touch—and scientific instruments that are extensions of the five senses, to explore and make sense of the world. But the logical mind is incapable of accessing anything nonmaterial. Only by using the intuitive mind's sixth sense can you connect with the more subtle energies associated with artistic creativity, spirituality, and wisdom. It is via the intuitive sense that you can plug into what Carl Jung called the collective unconscious, a vast body of knowledge that has been the source of all great insights and human advancements throughout the millennia.

Albert Einstein is an excellent example of the benefit behind blending the rational with the intuitive mind. As a physicist who created mathematical equations derived from fact and reason, he harnessed the power of the rational mind to explain his theories of relativity. But first it required the creative spark generated by the intuitive mind to stimulate his imagination sufficiently to allow him to formulate the insightful concepts that ultimately became the framework of his genius.

For most of us, our intuitive mind has become atrophied, shriveled up from lack of use. Parents often chastise their children for playing with imaginary friends or seeing a deceased loved one in their room after a funeral. Young children are still in touch with Invisible Energy, all that is intangible and ethereal, but quickly learn from adults to associate negative connotations with it. Our education system emphasizes using the rational mind to learn and usually gives less attention to non-cognitive activities.

My personal experience typifies this. Throughout my education, and especially in medical school, I was trained to rely on the rational mind and to use the scientific method to validate information. If new information could not be proved by scientific standards using double-blind, reproducible studies, it was not acceptable.

Because I appreciated the complexities of the human mind and its innate duality of logic and intuition, an internal struggle developed within me. My scientific mind understood the need to prove something as factual before using that information in my practice of medicine. But intuitive intelligence is not amenable to scientific authentication, given our existing state of technology. The scientific method of confirming new information cannot be applied to intuitive knowledge. We currently lack the necessary instruments to adequately measure and quantify the more subtle energies that our intuitive mind is able to perceive.

Parallel to my professional life, at a personal level, I began to explore my inner world of emotional and spiritual issues. Soon after graduating from medical school during my residency training I started meditating. In meditation, stimulation from the five senses is diminished, permitting the more subtle intuitive sense to become apparent. Meditation is an excellent technique for developing your ability to connect with your Higher self, your most trusted adviser in your endeavor to explore the spiritual lessons behind your suffering. Meditation is just one of several ways to enhance your intuitive abilities. Kinesiology, dreaming, intuitive flashes, and intuitive dialogue are other techniques that facilitate inner guidance, often connecting you with your inner wisdom more quickly than meditation. I discuss these methods in detail subsequently.

Beginning in my early years as a medical doctor, the knowledge I was acquiring in my training as a physician and surgeon was augmented by information I was perceiving through my sixth sense: intuition. As I applied this to my practice of medicine, a shift in my approach to caring for patients occurred. Diagnosing and treating illness took on a more gentle and humanistic quality. I began to spend more time with my patients, observing their body language and discerning the emotions behind their words. As I listened, a thought would suddenly appear in my head, an intuitive insight into a particular patient's problem. It could be what lab test or X-ray to order. Often it was clarity about the emotional stress that was causing the physical illness. Many times the diagnosis, or at least two or three possible diagnoses, would come to me. The scientist in me ordered the necessary test to confirm the diagnosis. The more I listened to my intuition, the stronger and more accurate it became. My intuitive mind became a valuable asset, enhancing the ability of my rational mind to facilitate healing.

My goal and intention in writing this book is to share information that will help you achieve improved health, greater happiness, and deeper spiritual insight into your pain and suffering. Although pain in your life is unavoidable, you do not need to feel overwhelmed or paralyzed by fear. You can take action to improve your situation. How do you accomplish this? It begins with a leap of faith – *everything happens for a reason*. Each painful experience, physical and emotional, is a co-creation by your self and your Higher self to provide an opportunity to bring your attention to the important lessons you need to be learning at this time. Rather than coming from a place of fear, you can use your intuitive ability to connect with your Higher self to figure out your lessons. Awareness of the underlying purpose behind your pain allows you to transmute suffering into personal and spiritual growth.

The biggest obstacle to success is doubt. Can I trust my ability to get accurate answers to the questions I pose to my Higher self? Can I rely on their validity? The tendency is to not trust yourself, but instead to defer to the opinion of others who you feel are authoritative and more knowledgeable. Of course you must acquire information from others to open yourself to new ideas and possible new solutions to resolve your difficulties. But it is essential that you personally plug in to *your* higher consciousness to confirm whether this information is pertinent to you. Others cannot give you your answers. They can only guide you in your search.

Although I have spent many decades exploring human suffering and have written this book to provide explanations for your personal dilemmas and possible solutions to help resolve them, I am not telling you to rely exclusively on me and assume that I have all the answers to your questions. ... I am telling you that *you* have the answers—for *you*. You will see that our "answers" are similar. Truth is truth. Regardless of our cultural or biological differences, connecting with that which is the source of knowledge and wisdom via our intuitive sense reveals a commonality that transcends human dissimilarities.

The accuracy of the information received through intuitively connecting with Invisible Energy is dependent upon the clarity of the individual attempting to perceive enlightenment. Your goal, therefore, is to become as clear as possible. The novice must patiently practice clearing his or her mind of distractions so as to enhance clarity. Meditation is an excellent tool for accomplishing this. With time, connecting with your intuition becomes automatic, making it always present whenever you want to use it. The more you use your intuition, the easier it will become to connect to it. After a while you will observe how often your intuition is correct, and you will feel confident in the validity of your sixth sense. You will appreciate the benefit of intuitive awareness in your life.

Throughout this book I use case histories of patients who demonstrate by example situations or lessons I am trying to highlight. Sometimes it is easier to see in others issues that are relevant to our own lives. I present their personal accounts so that you may benefit from their circumstances. To maintain patient confidentiality I have changed their names and other identifying details.

New ideas are presented in this book that will help you understand your pain and suffering. Keep in mind that everything worthwhile requires sacrifice. Releasing old paradigms of thought and behavior will feel uncomfortable, but your desire to reduce your physical and emotional pain will motivate you to overcome your inner resistance to change. Keeping an open mind and an open heart will enhance your personal healing.

CONSIDER THE POSSIBILITIES.

Chapter 1

Becoming

Where does a life's journey begin? At the physical level, sperm meets egg and we are born. Somewhere along the way, we realize another subtle, intangible aspect to our lives. Our consciousness is awakened; we search for answers. We begin a spiritual quest.

Becoming requires periodic life-altering experiences. As we evolve from nebulous masses of potential to actualized human beings, we go through stages of transformation throughout our lifetimes. During these challenging periods when circumstances hit us squarely between our eyes, we are compelled to consider questions we are ordinarily too busy to confront. Pain has a way of quickly getting our attention, shaking us free from the mesmerizing mundaneness of daily routines. Be it physical or emotional, pain is a strong signal that something is wrong. It may be ignored initially, persistent enough to seek medical assistance, or treated symptomatically, but eventually it will be serious enough to stop us dead in our tracks and begin the process of asking these kinds of questions:

> What's it all about?
> Why am I here?
> Is there a purpose to my life?

Is there a Higher Power?
Why is there so much pain?
Why is there so much suffering?
What happens when I die?

These are questions asked by a mind seeking meaning to one's life. It's getting the answers that's a bit tricky. They are not always readily apparent. We get so caught up in the pain and our desire to alleviate it that we are distracted from receiving the answers. Only by accepting the pain as part of life can anything positive come from the suffering. The choice is simple: grow and learn from the pain so that you may benefit; or ignore, blame, and feel victimized by it.

Pain is a necessary part of the human experience. Some people have more than others, but no one is spared. There is no avoiding pain. Trying to resist it only increases the suffering. Illness is a gift, not a curse. Unrequested to be sure, it is an opportunity for personal (mental and emotional) and spiritual growth. Illness is our teacher, sometimes benevolent in wanting to help us learn our lesson, and sometimes a taskmaster forcing us to face the unknown and wrestle with the challenges presented. The lessons offered by the occurrence of disease, or dis-ease, in our lives and the style in which we deal with them, reveal our degree of mastery of human melodrama. Because pain and aging are unavoidable, I urge you to embrace them. Determine the lesson to be learned, learn it (the hard part), and watch the suffering subside. While treating illness at the physical or psychological level with medication, counseling, body work, surgery, and so on, we can go beyond the limits of three-dimensional reality to identify and deal with the underlying growth issues being offered. We can choose awareness and growth over obliviousness and stagnation.

Becoming is ongoing. Spiritual growth develops as we progress from youth to maturity. Evolving brings a willingness to expand our spirituality by accepting the possibility of new concepts. Our viewpoint becomes transformed—beyond belief, beyond hope—to a place of knowing.

> I *believe* with my *mind*
> I *hope* with my *heart*
> I *know* with my *soul*

Faith is a bridge that allows us to cross over to the spiritual realm. For some of you, faith in a Higher Power is a given, a belief beyond the shadow of doubt. You are blessed. For the rest, uncertainty resides in the recesses of our minds. Only a leap of faith can catapult us over the abyss of doubt. Until and unless we can acknowledge energy beyond five-sense perception, we can progress no further in our spiritual exploration. Until and unless we understand that not everything we were taught is true, that there are possibilities previously not considered, the opportunity for growth will escape us.

My perception of truth includes a Higher Power. That term is vague in its connotation, which is my intention. The source of my spiritual guidance is not related to a specific religion, but rather to this amorphous energy that I, as a limited human being, cannot even begin to comprehend. God is a word most of us can relate to. Know that whenever I say God, I imply simultaneously Allah, Adonai, Ram, Lord, Grandfather, etc. Religion as a means to connect with Higher Power is no longer necessary for me. Anyone can plug into God consciousness without an intermediary. I view religion as a way for groups of human beings with similar values and beliefs to join in fellowship to connect with Spirit. I see religion and spirituality as mutually harmonious avenues toward individual spiritual growth. Each of us will find the right blend that suits our personal way of looking at the world. Take delight in your choice, allowing others to freely follow their own paths. It is all about love.

Higher Power, creator of all that exists, is so powerful that human beings would simply disintegrate if we actually "touched" God. We need our Higher self, the part of us that is capable of connecting with Higher Power, to receive intuitive guidance and wisdom. Each self, without exception, possesses a Higher self that knows God and all that is "God-ly." Our Higher self is always with us. It is a constant source of assistance as we deal with the issues or illnesses in our lives. By accessing Invisible Energy via our Higher selves, a connection is established that facilitates healing and provides spiritual insight.

Higher Power

↕

Higher self

↕

self

Beware of those who claim to know what's best for you. Indeed, our most worthy teachers are those who do not give us the answers but teach us how to find them. No one outside of ourselves can know our truth or determine the path we need to follow. Others can point us in a positive direction or illuminate possibilities previously unexamined, but ultimately we must look inward, trust our intuition, and know that our Higher self is the source of truth for us. If we learn how to plug in, we will have an ally for life.

Spiritual expansion implies transcendence from our ordinary reality. Life is filled with pain, suffering, boredom, and unpleasantness. Comfort is attainable, however. Help is available. To you. Yes, you. As you open yourself to new possibilities, the roadblocks to happiness and improved health are removed. Learning how to connect with your Higher self provides advice and wisdom when facing life's challenges. An intention is made to seek advice from your Higher self, and using techniques described in subsequent chapters, your answers will be forthcoming. Solutions to dilemmas and difficulties become apparent. There is less fear and more hope. You begin to experience moments of equanimity and serenity. Everyone is capable of plugging in. There are no exceptions. We are all equal in our opportunity to connect with our Higher self, and ultimately our Higher Power. It may be easier for some than others, but success will be achieved with concentration, determination, and patience.

Life minus Spirit equals Suffering

Life plus Spirit equals Hope

*   *   *

Have you noticed that everything is speeding up? We are in a period of expansion. New information and ideas are stretching our customary ways of viewing the world. Cosmically speaking, we are being caught up in a vortex of change. Everything is becoming more intense. Chaos is prominent. The written Chinese character for chaos combines two symbols representing both danger and opportunity, and that epitomizes this moment in history. What may appear scary at first can be seen instead with excitement. We are on the cutting edge of a shift in consciousness that requires us to be alert and aware. Being bombarded with rapidly transforming technology and current events makes it necessary for us to assimilate new information at a faster rate than our parents had to.

Just as the times are changing more quickly, so is the learning curve. Let's say it takes me twenty years to learn something. I teach it to person B. B learns it in ten years and then teaches person C. C learns it in five years and teaches person D, and so forth. We humans are capable of accelerated learning and growth when full attention is put to the effort. Change begins at the individual level. After a sufficient number of people accept the change as valid and real, it becomes generally agreed upon among the masses.

Ken Keyes Jr. relates the story of the hundredth monkey, which demonstrates how transformation on a large scale can occur quickly once critical mass has been achieved. He reports that scientists observing an island colony of monkeys saw one young member learn an efficient way to wash the sand from sweet potatoes. Starting with one innovative monkey, others gradually began to imitate the technique. Once the hundredth monkey learned it, it spread rapidly, within twenty-four hours, throughout the entire tribe. Mysteriously, this new concept was transmitted to other populations of monkeys on other islands many miles away. At some intangible level, knowledge was communicated between groups that was beneficial to all. Once an adequate, albeit not large, number of monkeys (or individuals) learns something, a sharing of information occurs that dramatically alters any previously accepted patterns of thought or behavior. Computers, books, magazines, television, and interpersonal networking are facilitating the shift. We are all part of it, whether consciously or unconsciously. You are not alone in your personal search for answers. Many of us see chaos permeating the whole planet, yet we hope, indeed intuitively know, that a higher purpose for human suffering exists.

Facing the pain of illness, whether our own or that of those we love—physical or emotional, acute or chronic, life threatening or life detracting—we have a need to make sense of it so that we may endure. Transcending the physical into the realm of the metaphysical, taking a leap of faith into the vagueness of that which human beings only partially understand, not only reduces suffering, but even more important, facilitates our souls' evolution to a Higher place. Regardless of the details of our individual lives, we are all here on this earthly plane with a common purpose. Each of us is a spiritual being on a human quest for knowledge and spiritual growth. We are here to learn about love.

Chapter 2

Pain

As a clinician I have witnessed terrible pain and suffering—physical pain that narcotic analgesics can barely relieve, and emotional suffering manifested as severe anxiety and suicidal depression. I have seen death come gently in one's sleep at the end of a long life, and I've seen it rob a ten-year-old child of experiencing a normal life span. Illness often has an unceremonious way of taking us by surprise, seemingly for no apparent reason, altering our lives forever.

Physicians and other caregivers face this daily. Learning how to cope with pain is essential for our emotional sanity and physical well-being. In moments of contemplation I have asked why pain is so integral to the human existence. Are we sinners and doomed to suffer? Are we foolish creatures bent on making self-destructive or unwise choices in life? Is there a God, and if so, why would a Higher Power allow so much pain?

My quest for an answer was rather fruitless at first. Observing my physician mentors, I tried the standard coping mechanism of detachment. Don't get too close. Shrugging my shoulders, accepting the belief that some questions are not meant to have logical answers, and avoiding asking the question worked for many years. When the pain became personal—my father's death—ignoring the issue was impossible. Why should I suffer, have difficulties, experience disappointments? I'm a good person. It's not fair. It just didn't make sense.

As a medical doctor trained to objectively assess information gathered by my five senses, computed through my logical brain to arrive at a rational explanation for observed phenomena, I felt ill equipped to tackle the philosophical issues of pain and death. My scientific mind could not provide the answers I was seeking. Coincidental to my personal search I began to notice an aspect to my practice of medicine that I hadn't paid much attention to previously, although it was always there. At some point during a medical workup an intuitive flash would come to me about a specific diagnosis or treatment. Experience has since taught me to notice my hunches and trust these gut feelings. The process of opening myself to my intuitive sixth sense facilitated greater clarity and insight. After a while the merging of the scientific with the intuitive resulted in my personal transition from physician to healer.

Life is composed of innumerable dualities: good/bad, day/night, male/female, and so on. Things are seldom black or white, but rather are shades of gray. The blending of the two aspects of any dyad is more powerful than either alone. Otherwise it becomes lopsided. Balance is the key. Not too much, not too little, somewhere in between. Within the context of health and illness, the joining of science and intuition results in more satisfactory healing. The best of both worlds. Merging the physical with the intangible.

With the conundrum of making sense of all the pain and suffering still looming before me, and dissatisfied with logical approaches, I resumed my quest by going straight to the Source. In meditation I asked, "Dear God, do you exist?" The answer I received was clear. I would have to spend more time being still to find out. I made a commitment to awaken earlier and extend my time with my Higher self and Higher Power to an hour or more every morning and five to ten minutes before lunch. I vowed to replace snatches of sleeplessness with actively connecting to Invisible Energy.

The biggest hurdle was doubt. It became apparent that nothing short of a leap of faith would allow me to accept the existence of an Energy, powerful and truly unknowable, that would make some sense of the painful difficulties all human beings experience. Time and contemplation provided access to intuitive confirmation of God's existence. In meditation, the response I received when asking about God's existence was clear:

The choice is yours to make

Because of inherent free will, each human being must make this decision independently. Since I reasoned that the existence of a Higher Power cannot be proved or disproved, the power of the rational mind was useless in this situation. All I could rely on was my intuition, my sixth sense. Quieting my mind and body allowed my five senses to be less dominant. Slow, deep breathing with eyes closed and body at rest permitted my conscious mind to recede, focusing instead on the subtle energy of the sixth sense. As I patiently repeated this process, asking for insight, and actively releasing doubt, a telepathic answer finally came to me:

Where love exists, fear cannot thrive
Where faith exists, doubt fades away

Doubt is relentless. Its constant presence can be overwhelming, closing our minds and hearts to new possibilities. Only by choosing to make the leap of faith to believe in something unprovable, just because it intuitively feels correct, can doubt be overcome. The pervasiveness of doubt makes belief in Invisible Energy an almost daily challenge. With time the strength of faith makes doubt less prominent. The existence of a Higher Power becomes truth, a genuine knowing, a daily presence, a constant companion.

Grappling with the issue of God's existence was difficult enough, but I was still left asking the original question. Why? Why the pain and suffering? Given that I choose to believe in a Higher Power, is this entity benign or vengeful? If it is vengeful, I and all of us are doomed to suffer. There is no hope there. Thus the second leap of faith presented itself. I decided to choose to believe that God cares about me, indeed loves me. The pure love from God is unconditional. Unlike parental love or religious blessing that requires me to be "good" before being rewarded with approval, I sense Higher love to be forthcoming no matter what. God's love for me is a constant. Can I prove this? No. Hence the leap of faith.

Doubt being the persistent nag it is, complete acceptance of God's existence and unconditional love for me, and for all living beings, does not come easily. To this day doubt still lingers, but less and less. As the doubt has been evaporating, replaced by a knowing, I have observed in myself the following changes: I am healthier, happier, and calmer. The more I connect with my Higher self, the less angry, worried, and sad I am. My suffering is diminished. Not that difficulties don't occur— they do so with ceaseless irregularity. What has changed is my *attitude* about the challenges being presented. The buoyancy of hope, inflated by God's love for me, has lessened my pains.

Pain. Why? With the question still unanswered, I continued to ask my Higher Power. One morning like a bolt of lightning the telepathic message became crystal clear:

The pain is here to facilitate growth

We are spiritual beings who have entered into physical form to have life experiences, each of which is designed to give us the opportunity to learn the lessons we need to promote our soul's growth. Soul has an existence unto its own. It merges with the physical, infusing the body with a life force, entering at the onset of life and departing at the time of death. Like all living entities, the purpose of the soul's existence is to grow. Trees, plants, and flowers reach for the sun. Among the animal kingdom the immature seek adulthood. Even our solar system and universe are expanding relentlessly outward. Growth.

We are individuated souls climbing an invisible spiral staircase to a higher place. We each have our own staircase, reaching upward toward a common goal— Source. We may climb quickly or slowly, or even slip and slide a bit, but overall the intention for each of us is to ascend at our own pace, each grappling with our own set of lessons to learn in this lifetime. *The purpose of our existence is spiritual evolvement and soul growth.*

And what is the impetus for this growth? Pain. Let's face it, when things are going great we humans sit back, relax, and enjoy the good times. It's when the pain hits us forcefully and unexpectedly that we stop and take notice. It's from the difficult and challenging times in our lives that most of us make the quantum leaps in our personal and spiritual growth, which ultimately is our reason for being.

If God exists and loves each and every one of us equally, why does our Higher Power sit idly by as we stumble wearily, burdened by life's troubles? The closest analogy I can make to help this be more understandable is to think of God like a parent watching his or her child learn to walk. The first time children fall and hit their heads, the parents don't whisk them into their arms and say, "There, there, I'll protect you and hold you in my arms so you don't ever have to walk and fall and hurt yourself again." Indeed, each time the children fall, the parents embrace them, kiss their pain, and then put them down and say, "Now walk." The process repeats itself, but always in the end, they say, "Now walk," encouraging the child to try again and again and again. God may wince at our tumbles and wish us only the very best, yet allow us to freely pursue our individual journey, as we must, back to the Light, back to the Godhead, our childlike arms reaching out toward the One.

Chapter 3

Illness

Illness, physical and psychological, is the major cause of human pain and suffering. Why do we become ill?

Homeostasis, where everything is in proper balance, is the norm. Good health and wellness are the natural state. All living things are programmed genetically to live a specific length of time. Human beings are designed to live approximately one hundred years given optimal conditions—avoidance of natural disasters or epidemics, living a healthy lifestyle, and good genetics. Yet few humans live this long. Those who do manage to live into their eighties or nineties are usually burdened by poor health, and are surviving in large part because of modern technological and pharmaceutical advancements.

Why is illness so prevalent, even among young, seemingly healthy individuals? Is there a reason why we are seeing so many more auto-immune diseases such as fibromyalgia and chronic fatigue syndrome cut people down in their prime? Why is the incidence of degenerative diseases such as hardening of the arteries (causing hypertension, heart attacks, and strokes), cancer, diabetes, and arthritis increasing in modern, developed societies?

There are four factors that influence a person's overall state of health: genetics, lifestyle, stress, and the immune system. Understanding how each affects one's health will give insight into how to better maintain optimum wellness.

*

Genetics begins to influence our lives from the moment of conception. All living things are made up of proteins, building blocks of amino acids that can be arranged in an infinite number of different patterns that form all biological matter. Genetics is the scientific investigation of how living organisms generate these essential proteins, and in the process create new life.

Contained within the strands of DNA chromosomes in each cell are the genetic templates, or blueprints, that determine the formation and function of every organ in our body. When we reproduce, we pass on genetic patterns of health that predispose us to be more susceptible, or resistant, to certain illnesses. This explains why smoking a pack of cigarettes a day can cause one person to develop lung cancer but not another.

Cancer often runs in families. Sometimes one specific organ tends to develop cancer, generation after generation. Other times what is inherited is a predilection toward cancer in general. In these situations, an individual can experience cancers in different organs when exposed to various cancer-causing agents that trigger the cellular mutations that lead to carcinoma. Therefore, of those who possess the genes for cancer, some will develop a cancer once, and others will have several organs form primary cancers over a lifetime.

> Frances began doing monthly self-examinations when her mother died of breast cancer at age seventy-six. Soon after Frances turned fifty-eight, she found a small lump in her left breast. It was diagnosed as intraductal carcinoma, and

early detection and a subsequent mastectomy saved her life. Although Frances was knowledgeable enough to alert her daughter to the "family curse," it came as a shock when her forty-year-old child informed her that a biopsy of a growth in her breast came back positive for cancer. Her daughter went on to have the breast removed and an implant inserted one year later. Lymph node biopsies were negative, and her daughter is doing well.

Cyrus was sixty years old when a suspicious nodule on his prostate was biopsied and diagnosed as cancer. He underwent a radical prostatectomy and remained free of cancer for fifteen years. Doctors use a laboratory test, prostate specific antigen (PSA), as a marker for advancing prostate cancer. When his PSA began to rise, it became apparent that a residual tumor recurred in the area of the prostate. He received extensive radiation to his pelvis that successfully destroyed the cancer. Unfortunately the beams of radiation also burned the surrounding tissues. Inflammatory colitis eventually turned into cancerous changes in the sigmoid colon, requiring surgical resection and a colostomy. Cyrus had always taken pride in being clean and neat. It took a while, but he eventually adjusted to having a bag attached to his abdomen to collect his stool. Three years later, blood appeared in his urine. A urological cystoscopy found cancer within the wall of the bladder. Now he had two bags to contend with, one for stool and one for urine. Around this time he came to me with a new growth on his arm. It had been enlarging rapidly for several months. The biopsy came back as melanoma, a potentially aggressive and lethal skin cancer. Wide surgical excision removed it completely from the arm. Unbeknownst to us, however, the melanoma had already spread by the time it was cut out. A year later, he noticed several bumps on his scalp. I biopsied one of them. Three days later, while awaiting the result, Cyrus had a seizure. He lapsed into a coma. A brain scan revealed multiple tumors. The next day the scalp biopsy came back: melanoma. The presumptive diagnosis of his brain cancers, therefore, was metastatic melanoma. He died two days later. In the last twenty years of his life, Cyrus experienced cancer of his prostate, colon, bladder, skin, and brain.

Another effect of genetics is its influence on how each of us reacts to stress. When we are emotionally distraught, or when we are working too hard without enough sleep to the point of physical exhaustion, illness ensues. Depending on genetic makeup, stress will cause one person to develop high blood pressure, another excess stomach acid, and someone else a migraine headache. Specific DNA markers will result in one part of the body being more prone to malfunctioning than others, causing a weak link that is more likely to break down during stressful times.

A family history of heart disease, cancer, or diabetes increases the likelihood of acquiring these maladies. However, not everyone with a predisposition to an inherited illness gets it. Other variables affect the final outcome, such as lifestyle choices, immune system vitality, environmental pollutants and toxins, and psychospiritual factors. The actual occurrence of these genetically predisposed disorders can be influenced by our free will, by the choices we make.

A new field of research called epigenetics is attempting to clarify exactly how lifestyle and stress influence genetics. Recent investigations reveal the existence of regulatory proteins within the nucleus of every cell that appear to coat DNA, thereby affecting DNA's ability to replicate or make new protein molecules. Ongoing research is indicating that environmental influences, as well as thoughts and feelings, affect the regulatory proteins. By so doing we can modify what was previously considered unalterable genetic control of our well-being. The implication of these biological experiments is that by choosing a healthier lifestyle and a more positive mental and spiritual attitude, we can offset our tendencies toward any specific genetically predisposed illness.

*

Lifestyle profoundly affects the quality of our health. We are accountable for the choices we make. There are natural consequences for what we eat, how often we exercise, our use of substances (nicotine, alcohol, caffeine, drugs), and the level of stress in our everyday lives.

Food is essential for life. We need the calories for energy, protein for repair and growth, and vitamins and minerals for proper cellular function. Glucose is the basic source of energy for every cell in the body. Glucose is gasoline for our engine. Whenever we need energy, our bodies break down sugar, starch, protein, and fat to glucose.

Our bodies handle the simple sugars in candy, soda, and sweetened foods differently from the complex sugars in fruits and vegetables. White flour is quickly converted to sugar by digestive enzymes in saliva, whereas whole grains are not. White sugar and white flour stimulate the pancreas to make much more insulin than fruit or whole grains. The excess glycemic response of simple sugar leads to diabetes, low blood sugar, elevated triglyceride levels, obesity, dental cavities, yeast infections, and hyperactivity.

Fats and oils are necessary ingredients in our diet. Animal sources of fat elevate cholesterol. Fish and fish oils, however, as well as vegetable oils, such as olive and flaxseed, are excellent sources of omega fatty acids that actually reduce the risk of strokes and heart attacks.

Salt in limited amounts is good for us and makes food more tasty, but in excess can lead to hypertension and fluid retention.

Choosing organic and natural foods promotes improved health by minimizing the harmful effects of pesticides, chemical fertilizers, hormones, and preservatives. The toxins in our food, water, and air pollute our entire body at the cellular level, resulting in malaise, fatigue, neuropathy, immune dysfunction, and cancer.

Eating food is one of life's greatest pleasures. Enjoying our food is important. The challenge for each of us is to consume healthful food that is satisfying as well. Sweet things taste good. Do we choose candy or fruit to snack on, soda or juice to drink? Do we eat foods made of enriched white flour (white bread, pasta, cake, cookies, piecrust, doughnuts, muffins, English muffins, bagels, sweet rolls), or do we select whole-grain breads and cereals, brown rice, and oatmeal instead? Fast foods are convenient, but are usually lower in nutritive value and fiber, and are filled with fat, salt, sugar, and chemicals.

The human organism is approximately 65 percent water: blood, lymph (the plumbing system that removes poisons and infections from the tissues of the body), digestive fluids, cerebral spinal fluid, and urinary tract fluid, plus all the water in and around every cell of the body. Fluid that does not move stagnates. Stagnant fluid putrefies and decays, causing illness and disease. It is important, therefore, to drink adequate amounts of fluids each day to keep well hydrated, and to exercise daily to keep our bodily fluids flowing.

Healthy people exercise regularly, four to seven times a week for at least thirty minutes. Aerobic activities prevent and alleviate hypertension, diabetes, osteoporosis, hyperlipidemia (elevated cholesterol and triglyceride fats), obesity, attention deficit disorder, anxiety, and depression. The older we get, the more prone we are to injury and the more slowly we heal. Stretching gently before and more fully after a workout prevents damage to muscles, tendons, and ligaments. When beginning an exercise program, it is advised that we start moderately and gradually increase both the length of time and the intensity of the work out. When we think of exercise as a fun activity, rather than a chore, the attitude of enjoyment becomes a key motivational ingredient.

Tobacco predisposes us to cancer, respiratory diseases, hypertension, and stomach problems. Alcohol can be harmful to anyone who has inherited an inability to adequately metabolize sugar, both causing and worsening diabetes, hypoglycemia, and emotional disorders. Alcoholism contributes to liver, stomach, and neurological disorders with often harmful consequences to interpersonal relationships. A fetus in utero is especially sensitive to tobacco, alcohol, and drugs, resulting in low birth weight, respiratory distress, fetal alcohol syndrome, birth defects, and seizures from drug withdrawal. Abuse of drugs can be devastating to anyone's physical and emotional health. Caffeine, the American drug of choice, when used to excess contributes to anxiety, insomnia, hypertension, tremors, breast tenderness, and digestive disorders.

Moderation is important in the prevention of illness. Most of us have bodies capable of withstanding small amounts of most things that are potentially harmful. The concept of moderation implies the avoidance of extremes. With food, too much or too little causes illness. Consuming too many calories leads to the development of obesity, diabetes, and cardiovascular diseases. Insufficient caloric intake, as seen in anorexia or bulimia, causes malnutrition. Whereas an inadequate amount of exercise promotes illness, embarking upon an exercise program too vigorously can cause musculoskeletal or heart problems. Most people can usually tolerate the modest use of caffeine and alcohol. Addictive substances, on the other hand, should be shunned to avoid the temptation and tendency toward overuse. For alcoholics, moderation is impossible, so abstention is advised. Cigarette smokers would suffer fewer respiratory problems if they smoked five cigarettes a day instead of a pack. Because nicotine is addictive, however, not smoking at all is best. Anything can become abused in people prone to excess, even something good such as food and exercise, so self-awareness is necessary if that tendency is part of your personality.

*

Stress, as much, if not more than any of the above excesses, is a causative agent in disease promotion. Research has clarified the intimate connection between our feelings and our physical health. *Psychoneuroimmunology* has given scientific credibility to the concept "As you think, so shall you be." A thought will trigger a feeling, causing the brain and nervous system to respond with certain chemicals, hormones, and neurological impulses that then have a direct effect on receptor sites in every organ of the body. Negative feelings release one set of molecules, and positive feelings release different ones. Anxiety, fear, and anger cause hormones, such as adrenalin, to overstimulate the body in a fight-or-flight reaction, adversely affecting the heart, nervous system, adrenal and other endocrine glands, and the immune system. Happy, loving, and other positive emotions release different hormones, chemicals, and neurological impulses. These have a calming effect on the important organ systems throughout the body, resulting in health-promoting biological activities instead of illness.

Stress can be external or internal. Be it at home, work, or both, we are frequently overwhelmed with too many external responsibilities, too many shoulds. We often have difficulty prioritizing the demands upon us, trying to do too many things in one day. By being so busy, we dissipate our energy outwardly in many directions. We become physically and emotionally drained of vigor and vitality. If we made time each day to relax or do something enjoyable, we would recharge our batteries and thereby avoid illness. But we often feel uncomfortable doing this. We learned from parents and other respected adults the importance of giving to others before attending to our personal needs. What was *not* modeled for us was the permission to give to ourselves. That was labeled selfish.

In fact, nurturing oneself is *self-loving*. The difference is that when one is selfish, one is getting one's needs met but hurting someone else in the process. With self-love no one else is harmed. We can put off a non-essential chore or obligation to energize our body, mind, or spirit. We feel we should do for others, but when we don't fill the well as it gets depleted, the well runs dry. If we don't nurture ourselves, we will get sick. Illness prevents us from helping anyone, others or ourselves. In the end, putting off self-loving activities leaves us still unable to meet the demands of others, and sick to boot! We were foolishly taught that it was acceptable to get out of duties and responsibilities because of illness, but not because we were taking the time for self-caring activities, or *inactivities,* that are health promoting. Our priorities have become distorted such that we too often choose acquiring money or fulfilling obligations over seeking happiness or equanimity.

It is internal stress, however, that insidiously affects our health in an even more harmful way. Negative self-talk is an ever-present reminder of how unworthy we consider ourselves. "I'm not good enough" is an unconscious mantra harping on our psyche, judging our every action, word, and thought. Feelings of inadequacy undermine the natural tendency toward wellness. Through the mind-body connection, defense mechanisms designed to protect us and thereby contribute to optimal health are broken down, resulting in illness.

*

The part of the body most sensitive to the effects of stress is the immune system. This protective network of lymph glands, spleen, thymus gland, and white blood cells forms the defense system of the body. The thymus gland is a tiny organ near the heart that coordinates the white blood cells as they travel throughout every part of the body, seeking out and destroying anything considered foreign to the individual. Specifically, it is the protein of the foreign material that alerts the surveillant white blood cells.

Any protein can trigger an immune response if its DNA pattern is different from our own. The source of this foreign protein can be from outside the body or from within, external or internal. Given exposure to a foreign protein, the immune system is capable of responding in one of two ways—it can underreact or overreact. The following chart, which I modified from *The Healer Within* by Steven Locke, MD, and Douglas Colligan, shows the four types of illness that can result from immune dysfunction.

IMMUNE RESPONSE

	Under Reactive	Over Reactive
External	Infection (microorganism)	Allergy (allergen)
Internal	Cancer (malignant cell)	Auto-immune (viral/organ complex)

External proteins include microorganisms, which cause infections, and allergens, which cause allergies. Internal proteins contain some of our DNA, but in a mutated way that is altered sufficiently to be considered foreign to the immune system, like malignant cells (cancers) and viral/organ complexes (auto-immune diseases).

Our immune system is constantly vigilant. Once a scout white blood cell detects an unfamiliar protein, it signals the thymus gland to mobilize killer white blood cells to surround the abnormal protein and engulf it. This protective process happens naturally without our awareness. We are exposed to germs all the time and yet do not usually become ill. Our immune system destroys the invading microorganisms whenever we are exposed to them. We become sick only if we are inundated with a large dose of virulent microorganisms, or if we are so stressed that our immune system fails to function adequately. Scientific studies repeatedly demonstrate that negative emotions, such as anger, fear, stress, or depression, adversely affect our immunity by paralyzing the white blood cells and interfering with their function to destroy abnormal proteins such as germs and cancer cells. Anger and fear result in adrenal gland stimulation, causing adrenalin and cortisol to be secreted. Adrenalin gives us the energy to do battle. Among the effects of cortisol is suppression of the immune response to foreign proteins.

Given that there are trillions of cells in every adult human organism, any random genetic mutation can result in the formation of a cancer. We all develop cancerous growths many times in our lifetime. Our immune system usually destroys these aberrations at the microscopic level as soon as they appear, without our realizing it. It's not until we experience major stress or depression that our immune system is compromised, allowing a dangerous cancerous tumor to grow unimpeded.

Resentment is one of the most common feelings that leads to immune suppression. When we are very upset about something someone close to us does, but for whatever reason are not comfortable expressing our anger directly to them, we internalize these strong emotions. Resentment sufficient enough to result in cancer comes from a deep wounding to our psyche. Repeated hurt or abuse for many years festers inside us. Often, fear of physical or emotional retaliation prevents us from expressing our feelings honestly. Ultimately this will cause a spontaneously occurring cellular mutation to blossom into a malignancy, unchecked by our immune system. We feel so much anger and resentment that we literally eat ourselves up alive.

Looking at the immune response chart, we see that the immune system strongly influences two other areas of health: allergies and auto-immune diseases. These two categories of illness share a different immune dysfunction—an overactive hyper-reaction to a foreign protein. With infection and cancer, the immune system is *underreactive,* not responding adequately enough, allowing either germs or cancer cells to take over the organism. With allergies and auto-immune illnesses, our immune system is *overreactive*, either to an external protein (allergen) as in the case of allergy, or to an internal protein (virus/organ complex) as in auto-immune disorders.

Allergens can be airborne pollens, animal dander, dust mites, foods, or chemicals, all of which stimulate the immune system to overreact. Any noxious irritant will trigger an exaggerated response called an allergic reaction. Bee stings, organ transplants, and mistyped blood transfusions can also cause this reaction.

Auto-immune diseases include lupus, rheumatoid arthritis, thyroiditis, Type I juvenile diabetes, fibromyalgia, and chronic fatigue syndrome/CFIDS. In these conditions a virus enters the body with a predilection for a specific organ. A physically *or* emotionally stressed immune system does not mount an adequate initial response to this germ. The virus attacking its target organ goes on to form an inflammatory reaction within the specific organ. Eventually this virus/organ complex does stimulate the immune system. This results in the white blood cells attempting to destroy not only the offending microorganism, but also the organ it is adhered to. Ultimately the organ itself is slowly destroyed by a misguided immune system. Auto-immune conditions are therefore chronic, difficult to cure by conventional means, and often very debilitating.

*   *   *

Health is an outward manifestation of a holistic balance and harmony within the heart, mind, body, and spirit. The heart represents our feelings, the mind our thoughts, the body the physical, and the spirit the spark of Divinity within each of us. Health will be attained as a result of a full expression of both the positive and negative aspects to each of the four components, balanced in a manner that avoids excessiveness. Taking a holistic approach to why we become ill will further clarify the causes of illness.

*

HEART. A healthy heart results from being completely in touch with the full range of human emotions. All feelings can be broken down to two primary emotions—love and fear. From love comes joy, happiness, gratitude, serenity, and good health. From fear comes anger, hatred, jealousy, prejudice, war, and illness.

Anger is a secondary emotion, with fear at the core of all anger. When anger is triggered by a person or situation, the healthy individual recognizes the feeling, acknowledges it rather than denies it, and resists the temptation to either express it outwardly in a hurtful way or repress it internally as guilt or self-loathing.

A feeling of anger in any present moment situation is actually the result of tapping into a *past* fearful experience such as abandonment, abuse, loneliness, punishment, or judgment. These deep wounds need healing. If we see our anger as a reflection of our inner pain, we can address an old emotional trauma each time anger alerts us to it. By doing this repeatedly, over many years, we emerge on the other side, forgiving the perpetrator of our childhood fearful experience or abuse, and ourselves for thinking it was our fault. The people who cause us the greatest pain and difficulties are our most important teachers, illuminating for us the primary issues that we need to address in this lifetime.

> Carol gets angry with her husband whenever he makes a comment that she feels is critical. One evening he made a passing remark that dinner was delicious but a bit too salty. Carol got so upset that she grabbed his plate, threw the food in the garbage, and shouted, "If you don't like my cooking, you can get takeout tomorrow!"

Carol's mother was a perfectionist. Whenever Carol was learning something new, her mom would eagerly help her, but always in a way that made Carol feel that although her efforts were good, they were not quite good enough. In a pleasant voice, her mother would always find something to improve. "That's very nice, dear, but if only you would ..."

All this came out coincidentally when I saw Carol and her husband after a motor vehicle accident. She was driving, they were rear-ended, and it was not her fault. As he was explaining the details, she suddenly got very defensive and yelled at him. Her husband confided that she did this all the time. It was during the next follow-up visit, when I brought up her inappropriate emotional reaction, that she told me about her mother and her childhood. Once Carol realized the root of her sensitivity to being controlled or criticized, she began to be less hard on herself, and those around her.

The effect of fear is to undermine the well-being and health of ourselves or others. Love, on the other hand, enhances the nurturing environment that promotes good self-esteem and positive feelings of self-worth. When faced with a fearful situation or feelings of fear within us, a simple exercise can turn our emotions in a more positive direction. We can use our free will and our freedom of choice to choose love over fear. When we observe ourselves being afraid or negative, we can ask a simple question: "Would I rather be coming from a place of fear or would I rather be coming from a place of love?" Naturally we prefer love, so we can then ask, "What would be the loving thing to do in this situation?" We can actively use the power of our intention to change our behavior or our thinking toward a more positive or loving option.

When Stephanie's sixteen-year-old daughter Ashley asked her for permission to go on her first date, Stephanie's first reaction was to say no. She imagined her beautiful child being raped, maimed, or killed, and felt a maternal need to protect her. Naturally, Ashley protested. "Don't you trust me? You taught me right from wrong, Mom. I'll be careful, I won't drink, and I promise not to drive with anyone who has been drinking." Stephanie realized Ashley was going to start dating eventually, and that she was basically a responsible and levelheaded kid. She had taught her daughter how to drive as soon as Ashley turned sixteen, so Stephanie knew Ashley could drive if her date couldn't. Being a responsible parent, she asked Ashley about the boy and his family. Stephanie expressed her fears for Ashley's safety and listened while her daughter reassured her. Despite her fears, Stephanie consented. Her daughter gave her a big hug, proud that her mother trusted her. They compromised and agreed on a curfew. The night of the date arrived. The two of them laughed as Ashley put on her make-up and got dressed. It was a shared special moment for both of them.

In the end Stephanie was very happy that she had put her worries aside. She realized that the most loving decision was to allow her child to freely live out her life so she could learn her valuable life lessons. There comes a time when every parent has to let go of control and have faith. After Ashley left on her date, Stephanie prayed to her Higher Power to watch over and protect Ashley. She reasoned that God was more powerful than she was, and because she couldn't be by her daughter's side to protect her, God would be a wonderful surrogate. By putting her trust in God, and her child, Stephanie was able to transform fear into love. As a result, her daughter appreciated her mother's confidence in her, and decided to make sound choices herself so she could rise to the level of her mother's positive expectations.

Achieving balance in the expression of feelings is ideal. Taking either of the primary emotions—love and fear—to an extreme will lead to undesirable outcomes. Inadequate love can manifest as child neglect, marital coldness, self-destructive behaviors, and overindulgences. Excessive expressions of love present as overprotectiveness, codependency, and pity. Too much fear causes anger, verbal or physical abuse, and bigotry. Insufficient fear can result in excessive risk-taking behavior, and cause danger to ourselves and all we are responsible for protecting.

*

MIND. Events that occur in our everyday lives can trigger memories or thoughts. Past experiences influence how we react to current situations. If the past incident was a good one, the thought and subsequent feeling will be positive. If the memory was a bad one, we will unconsciously register negativity in our mind and heart. Take for example our reaction to having a dog we don't know approach us. If we are familiar with dogs or had them as childhood pets, we will be careful but not afraid. If we've had a scary experience with a dog in the past, our reaction will be fearful.

Harboring negative thoughts about ourselves or others is a consequence of a judgmental attitude. We were told so often as youngsters that we were not good enough that our tendency as adults is to act on that false belief. Negative self-talk is a subliminal dialogue that undermines our self-esteem. We then project those judgmental thoughts onto others, and with accusations or actions, we perpetuate the negativity—us to them and them back to us. Sometimes saying or doing something hurtful can cause a chain reaction that passes from one person to another, to then another, and so on.

> Bernie is a dog. He was part of a family camping next to us. There was a mom and a dad, a ten-year-old girl, a seven-year-old boy, and Bernie. Dad came back to camp

upset about a frustrating experience he had had in town and began to complain to Mom for sending him on the errand. Five minutes later Mom chastised her daughter for not washing the dishes from breakfast. As the little girl got up and walked past her brother, she pushed him out of her way and called him a jerk. When Bernie started barking at a passing dog, the little boy ran up to him, shouting for him to be quiet, and kicked him. Dad to Mom to daughter to brother to Bernie. I call it the Bernie syndrome. Cascading anger from one, to another, to another.

The clinical manifestations of excess negative thinking are anxiety and depression. Self-doubt leads to feelings of unworthiness. Life becomes overwhelmingly fearful when we feel inadequate to cope with the difficulties and pains that befall us. Repeated self-criticism is the main psychological cause for depression (grieving for loss being the other). It requires many decades, if not an entire lifetime of emotional and spiritual healing before we can eventually accept that indeed we are each a beautiful child of God, worthy of God's love. Our greatest challenge is to love our self as much as God loves us—unconditionally.

Attitude is another strong factor in determining the degree of negativity or positivity we feel in response to an event in our lives. Some people have a sunnier disposition, go more easily with the flow, and naturally prefer to put a more positive spin on things that happen to them. Others approach life with suspicion, ready to see the negative consequences, fearful of harmful outcomes. Regardless of natural tendencies, our free will allows us to choose to override any negative thought with a more hopeful one.

Behavior modification is an excellent technique for attitudinal adjustments, or for changing any behavior we no longer want to continue. This three-step process initially requires awareness of the negative thought or repetitive habit we want to change. Using our willpower, we stop our thought or behavior, replacing it consciously with a more positive one.

1. *Awareness* of thought or behavior
2. *Stop* it
3. *Change* it

What at first seems like a cumbersome process eventually becomes easier and faster. Although bad habits are hard to break, the more positive reaction eventually becomes second nature.

> One day I came home after a difficult day at work to find my daughter and our two dogs running through the house. I abruptly yelled at her, "Take the dogs and go outside!" A few minutes later, as the three of them were playing, the dogs started barking incessantly, prompting me to open the door and shout, "Stop making so much noise!" After I made a third negative comment later that evening, my daughter turned to me and said, "Daddy, why are you yelling at me so much?"
>
> 1. Awareness: Jeff, you're taking your stress out on Tara.
> 2. Stop: I apologized and went into the study.
> 3. Change: I took ten slow, deep breaths with my eyes closed. Five minutes later I rejoined my family, feeling calmer and less irritable.

With the power of the mind and through the willful decision to dwell more on the positive than the negative, a transition gradually occurs. The conscious shifting of energy toward the affirmative causes a cascade of more positive feelings to emerge, which, through the pathway of psychoneuroimmunology, results in improved health. In some cases the healing process can progress rapidly. In other cases, years may be required to achieve optimal health.

At the interpersonal level this shift results in more harmonious relationships at home and at work. It is amazing how our thoughts are transmitted telepathically to other people. A conscious transformation *within* us has an external influence on those *around* us. All of us have the power to alter the level of energy in others, up or down, with the intensity of *our* thoughts.

Recently I have been experimenting with telepathic communication. One of my projects has been to see if I could transmit a thought to another person. Because I drive seventeen miles each way between my home and my office, mostly on the freeway, I decided to experiment with other drivers on the road. Having a Type A personality, I prefer the left-hand lane when driving in traffic. In the past, if I came upon a slow driver, I would get upset and pass them. I began to randomly choose, instead, one of two options. Half the time I would simply stay a safe distance behind the slow driver and not think any thoughts about them, positive or negative. Usually they continued driving slowly, oblivious to my being behind them. The other half of the time, as soon as I came upon them, I would look directly at the backs of their heads and think, *Please speed up or move over. Please speed up or move over. Please speed up or move over. Thank you.* I was amazed at how quickly they either moved over or sped up once I did that—within seconds, most of the time. Uncanny. Approximately 20 percent of the time, the other driver, immersed in deep thought or on a cell phone, would be too distracted to perceive my telepathic thought. But the vast majority of the time the process works successfully.

Unbeknownst to my wife, I have also been experimenting with telepathic communication between the two of us. Rather than tell her or ask her something, I would just think it. Surprisingly, Patty would spontaneously bring up the subject on her own, seemingly out of the clear blue. Sometimes it was reversed where I would intuitively start talking about something and she would comment that she had just been thinking about that subject herself. Over time, this has been occurring more frequently and more consistently between us. Another area of telepathic communication that fascinates me is healing from a distance. Can a group of people, or even one individual, send healing energy to another person resulting in improvement of their condition? Researchers are currently exploring this concept.

> Before a wildfire destroyed part of the forest and brush surrounding our group of homes fifteen years ago, the path I took on my daily walks often passed two herds of deer—mule ear and white-tailed. To avoid spooking them as I came upon them, I would matter-of-factly continue on the trail, avoiding stopping and staring at them. I glanced at them sideways only to gaze at their natural beauty, and repeated silently, telepathically, as I walked past them, *I love you, I won't hurt you. I love you, I won't hurt you, I love you, I won't hurt you.* For years the deer and I coexisted peacefully, enjoying together the quiet of the early morning.

*

Physiologically, when the brain is studied using advanced neuroimaging technology, it can be demonstrated that a specific thought, positive or negative, results in reproducible stimulation to localized areas in the cerebral cortex and midbrain. These neuroelectric firings go on to produce hormonal and neurochemical reactions that result in specific emotions such as fear or happiness. The mind, therefore, directly influences our feelings. The thoughts we generate, conscious *and* unconscious, determine the emotions we experience.

But what initiates the thought? Acknowledging that a thought will result in an emotional reaction, and that that particular feeling will have direct effects on our physical body, the question that arises is, what precedes the thought?

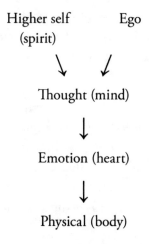

Higher self   Ego
(spirit)

Thought (mind)

Emotion (heart)

Physical (body)

The positive thoughts are generated by our Higher self, the part of us that is connected to Spirit. The source of negative thinking is our ego.

Born egoless, we develop this psychic armor to safeguard ourselves from the pains of life. From infancy on, each painful experience wounds us. The natural response to being hurt is to be afraid. We don't want to be hurt again, so our psyche responds to the emotional and physical assaults by developing coping techniques to protect itself from the next attack. Motivated by fear, the ego's guard goes up whenever it senses danger. Learned self-protective behaviors are initiated to shield us.

When we feel threatened, we respond in one of several ways. We may respond to the fearful situation with anger, lashing out at anyone we feel is attacking us. Or we may have learned that it is easier or safer to be passive and allow the abuse to occur without much resistance. Or we may choose denial, preferring to stuff our feelings into our subconscious mind rather than address the pain consciously in the present moment.

Anger is an appropriate emotion when we feel attacked. If we're not comfortable expressing our anger directly at the perpetrator of the pain, we direct it inwardly instead. Rather than attacking someone else, we attack ourselves. Suppressed anger manifests as self-attack or self-criticism. Our ego judges ourselves as bad, blaming ourselves instead of the other person.

As children our self-esteem becomes undermined by repeated assaults to our psyche, so our developing egos begin to think of ourselves as inadequate and deserving of punishment. The result of all this incessant negative self-talk is to influence our thoughts to be critical of ourselves. Whereas our Higher self loves us unconditionally, our ego judges and condemns us. Over time, repeated self-punishment leads to depression.

Our ego develops to protect us from pain. Because pain is inherent to life, and therefore unavoidable, the ego is faced with a dilemma. Sensing an inability to protect us, our ego feels powerless and out of control. It worries about imminent danger and becomes anxious. In its desire to cope with fruitless attempts to protect us from the hardships of life, the ego responds by adding layer upon layer of defensive armor.

In the end, however, rather than protect us, our ego's defense armor actually insulates us from others. Ego-protective defenses necessary in childhood become cumbersome when we are adults, interfering with healthy interactions with significant others in our life. We build up a wall of neurotic thoughts and behaviors that no longer serve us, but instead imprison us in a cocoon of fear. No one can get in ... but then, we can't get out, either. We feel so vulnerable that we are afraid to take the risk of being open to others. Out of fear that someone will hurt us, we withdraw inward. This prevents us from reaching out to others and receiving the love and nurturance necessary to heal our childhood wounds. We choose safety over happiness. Fear continues to dominate our emotions, further enlarging our ego and its ineffective armor of protection. Despite the efforts of our ego, however, pain persists.

Free will is the human ability to choose one course of action over another. With every thought we have, we can decide whether our ego or our Higher self will be the predominant influence on our subsequent thoughts and actions.

When ego prevails, in any situation or interaction with another person, we react defensively in our attempt to protect our self from being hurt. When we allow Spirit, through our Higher self, to enter the picture, the outcome is less scary and more harmonious.

> You are walking down a street and someone else is coming toward you. You assess whether this person is a potential threat to you by observing his or her body language and other visual cues. You can react in one of two ways. Depending on your previous life experiences, your fear-driven ego may initially generate a neurochemical fight-or-flight fear reaction in your brain. If instead of relying exclusively on your ego, you choose to also connect intuitively with your Higher self, you then have the option to not automatically react with fear. Detecting no danger signals, and having determined that the situation is safe, you can choose to have Spirit guide your thoughts. The natural inclination of your Higher self is to come from love. As you pass the other person, you decide to smile or nod. Most likely that person will also respond in a friendly manner.

The balanced mind strives for excellence, all the while acknowledging that every human makes mistakes. We can never learn from our mistakes if we don't make any. The healthy individual is able to be lighthearted enough to accept his or her personal foibles and still feel good about having done his or her best.

*

BODY. A healthy body possesses the strength and flexibility to perform all necessary activities of daily living and is able to perform all physiological functions without difficulty or pain. These internal activities include circulation, respiration, digestion, elimination, and procreation. Achieving balance of the physical is most conducive to good health. A balanced diet of lean protein, complex carbohydrates, and polyunsaturated fats, that is low in sugar, salt, and refined white flour, and liberally augmented with fruits and vegetables, is ideal. Drinking eight glasses of fluid daily provides sufficient liquid for optimal bodily functions. Because both caffeine and alcohol have a dehydrating effect on the body, it is advised to follow each caffeinated or alcoholic beverage with a glass of water. A balanced exercise regimen includes stretching the entire body to limber the muscles, tendons, ligaments, and joints, combined with daily aerobic exertion for at least thirty minutes for cardiovascular benefits.

Sleep is required for healing and growth. Physical and emotional health benefit from adequate rejuvenation. Insomnia caused by physical pain, frequent urination, or indigestion is the body's way of signaling the need for medical assistance. Both anxiety and depression cause insomnia. Difficulty falling asleep results from anxious rumination, whereas awakening early around 3:00 a.m. may be a sign of depression.

*

SPIRIT. A healthy spirit allows one to have the faith to go beyond believing to a place of knowing. There is an appreciation for one's personal connection to Spirit. When we are well balanced, we see our place in the overall scheme of things. We see that we are simultaneously both a speck of sand on the beach of life ... and a precious child of God. A healthy spirit provides perspective, an appreciation for the beauty in the world as well as an understanding of the need for pain to promote growth.

Happiness comes from something or someone outside of our self that gives us pleasure. Joy comes from within, not because of any external event or person, but as a spontaneous manifestation of gratitude. Serenity comes from our personal connection to our Higher Power, a gift derived from a healthy spirit. Trusting in a higher purpose to our existence allows us to give up resistance to the occurrences in our lives, even the unpleasant ones, giving us faith that everything is happening for a reason. Understanding that the reason is our spiritual growth facilitates the experience of serenity or bliss. Spiritual balance allows us to make sense of all the pain and suffering, to give us peace of mind. It is our lifeline as we drift through our existence, reminding us that we are never alone.

It is easier to touch Divinity when sitting alone on a mountain top. The challenge is maintaining what we learn from Spirit while mingling amidst all the temptations of the material world. Seeking spiritual enlightenment brings us to lofty heights of idealism, wonderful at times, but if unbalanced, not conducive to practical dealings in the physical world. Having our heads in the clouds leaves the rest of the organism vulnerable. Therefore, the perfect balance of spirit and material requires a combination of idealism and practicality.

Raising children provides an excellent example of the need for this balance. Children require frequent demonstrations of love to provide a nurturing environment to stimulate positive growth. Without firm and consistent boundaries, however, a child can suffer harm or become undisciplined. Tough love is the balance that offers a child the best opportunity for maximum self-realization.

*   *   *

Why do bad things happen to good people? Despite good genetics and healthy lifestyle choices, illness still occurs. It is unfair and illogical. Yet disease and pain happens to all of us. Why? Is it random circumstance that calamity touches us all? Perhaps. If so, it is completely beyond our control, so nothing can be done. If there is no Higher Intelligence orchestrating or influencing our destiny, no rhyme or reason for our suffering, then there is no sense even trying to change or improve our life. This is how the seeds of victimhood, sprouted from the soil of powerlessness, take root, planting us firmly in the ground, immobile and unable to release ourselves from eternal suffering.

Instead, one can choose to believe that a Higher Power does exist, and indeed is the personification of love, benevolence, and wisdom. When the question is again asked why there is so much pain and illness, why a loving God would allow suffering to befall all human beings, at least two possible answers come to mind.

Many see God as an omniscient parent, loving us but also teaching us right from wrong. Punishment is sometimes a necessary part of this process. Illness is sometimes viewed as retribution for our sins, the natural consequence of being imperfect. However, if God is the Unity that encompasses all conceivable dualities, the sum total of all that exists, the epitome of unconditional love, then punishment becomes truly incongruent. Besides, I get no solace from believing that I am so unworthy that God would want to punish me.

Indeed, we are spiritual beings in possession of a soul that existed before we were born. Our souls choose to incarnate in physical form so that we may have life experiences, all of which are designed to give us the opportunities to learn the lessons that our soul needs in its evolution. Our soul, drawn toward or actively seeking the Light, desires to learn the lessons that will make it more complete, more perfect. Each person has his or her own set of lessons to deal with in life. Your lessons are not the same as mine, and are not the same as those of a two-year-old child starving to death in Darfur. We each have different situations in our lives that present us with the opportunities to learn our specific set of needed lessons.

This is earthschool. We are here to learn. Although school is not necessarily enjoyable, it is essential. At any one moment in time, we are each in different classrooms, but eventually we must take all the required classes before graduation from the birth-death cycles of life. The concept of earthschool, which my wife introduced to me during a conversation many years ago, clarifies the purpose behind human existence.

Our lessons are often presented to us through pain. It is from the difficult times that we face our demons, confront our fears and doubts, and, ideally, come through to the other side having satisfactorily learned the lessons being offered. Pain and illness, therefore, become gifts—unpleasant to be sure, but essential to stimulating us to deal with our issues so that we may achieve personal and spiritual growth. Illness teaches us strength, persistence, and patience. It teaches us to endure pain. For healers, it is an opportunity to serve humankind.

Scientific confirmation of the concept of earthschool is challenging. Hypnosis, a psychological technique used for more than a hundred years to access the deeper regions of the mind that lie behind conscious thought, has been used recently to explore metaphysical ideas such as this. One application of hypnosis is regressive hypnosis, a method used to bring a person back in time, while hypnotized, to a previous circumstance requiring in-depth exploration (for example, a dog bite or molestation). In the last several decades a few therapists have expanded this technique to regress individuals beyond childhood traumas, back to their birth, back to the womb, and back further.

It was a patient who first introduced me to the research published by Michael Newton, PhD, in his book *Journey of Souls*. As a psychologist who used hypnosis in his treatment of patients, he began using past-life regression to explore what, if anything, precedes our birth into this life. His research has shown that before the soul fuses with the body, there is a process whereby the soul, or Higher self, chooses the basic framework of a life that will provide the best circumstances for illuminating the important issues needing to be addressed in this existence. Time is relative. Past, present, and future are arbitrary delineations necessary only in three-dimensional reality. The fourth dimension transcends time. During the process of picking the most appropriate life to achieve soul growth the soul *pre-views* the major life events that will be necessary to generate growth—including the painful ones.

Therefore, at a subconscious soul level, our Higher self will choose to enter a body knowing full well ahead of "time" the painful life events that will create the opportunities for growth. Because we choose, at a spiritual level, the challenging circumstances in our lives, there is no place for feeling sorry for ourselves. Being a victim is impossible if we are a co-creator of our own life—co-created by our self and the choices we make, and our Higher self and the lessons needed for soul growth.

Scientists are explorers. We observe the world and then try to make sense of it. Learning is often best achieved through personal experience. Reading about past-life regression sounded fascinating, but I had to know firsthand whether to trust its validity. Knowledgeable about using hypnosis to get past the rational mind to connect with the intuitive mind, I decided to allow myself to be regressed twice. As a result of these past-life regressions, and a few very insightful deep meditations, I have personally experienced glimpses into several of my past lives. During one of the sessions, while I was under hypnosis, the psychologist asked me why I had chosen to enter my current body. The question prompted an immediate "memory" of choosing to enter the fetus that would develop in my mother's uterus. I then suddenly remembered that before this current life I had chosen to be the embryo she had miscarried in her *previous* pregnancy. Having missed that opportunity, my soul chose her next conception.

Interestingly, the body of the person I would have been had my mother not miscarried her first pregnancy would have been physically different from my current one, but my soul would have been the same—mine. My mother, early in her pregnancy with me, threatened to miscarry again. She was given medication to prevent that from happening. It worked, obviously, but it caused some physical changes in my body that are different from the body that would have resulted from her first pregnancy. I "saw" that body, as an adult, while under hypnosis, and it was quite different from my current one. But I needed to be raised by the two people who are my parents—if not in one body, then another.

We choose our parents intentionally. They are among our most important teachers. Parents often teach by reverse example. Often we observe them and vow to be just the opposite. We even choose the abusers. Keep in mind, this is all occurring at a subconscious, soul level. As distasteful as pain is to our physical being, to our soul it is the springboard for spiritual growth.

Once the soul and body fuse, they never completely separate until death. During times of unconsciousness the soul remains connected. Sleep, deep meditation, or even coma do not sever this umbilical cord–like attachment. Near-death experiences maintain a definite, albeit tenuous, connection. Such an experience, where all vital functions of circulation and respiration cease and the individual is then resuscitated with eventual resumption of these functions, must by definition keep intact the threadlike soul-body union. Returning from near-death experiences necessitates restoring the soul to a completely intact bond with its physical home.

Near-death events have life-altering consequences for those fortunate to survive. As with all painful or challenging circumstances in our lives, the intent is growth through experience. Difficulties give us the opportunities to evolve. The awareness we achieve upon analysis of the meaning behind these occurrences or illnesses is the impetus to propel us upward as we ascend our individual spiral staircases to a Higher Place.

*   *   *

Life is a co-creation. Our self and our Higher self both influence the unfolding of our life. The energy that affects our life choices is called will. There is personal will and Divine will. Personal will is that which we, our self, our ego, wants. Divine will implies a decree by God, but in actuality the source of Divine will is dual: Higher Power and Higher self. Our Higher self, or soul, took on physical form to learn important lessons. God and soul made an agreement before birth. At a spiritual or subconscious level, a "contract" was agreed upon, forming the framework or blueprint of our existence. As a result of this agreement certain things will need to happen in our life to set up the scenarios that force us to make choices that ultimately determine the extent to which we achieve awareness and growth in this lifetime.

Inherent in the human condition is freedom of choice. Life is a series of choices. Many times every day we are placed in situations where we can choose a more positive option versus a more negative one. The choice we make determines which outcome will occur. Therefore, as a result of our choices, we affect the reality we create.

Divine will and free will. Predetermined agreements and choices we make. Co-creation.

Things happen to us that we, our selves, do not want to happen. What appears from our human perspective to be happening beyond our control is actually occurring deliberately, and definitely with our consent … the consent of our Higher self. Ordained by our Higher Power and our Higher self, decisions were made before our physical self was ever born. These agreements are spiritual in nature, below the conscious level of thinking, and are therefore without the ego's awareness. Once determined before birth, they are set. When the self wants something—that is, personal will—that desire is sometimes thwarted. If there is a conflict between what the ego-driven self wants and what is in our spiritual best interest, what we want to happen will not occur. There is a bigger picture. Any prearranged agreement will take precedence, and whatever is necessary to achieve spiritual growth must play itself out. Hence, Divine will dominates over our personal desires. Divine will always supersedes personal will.

As a consequence of these agreements, much of what happens to us in earthschool is beyond our ego's control. What is within our control, however, is how we choose to *react* to the events or people in our life. It is by virtue of the choices we make, with the power of our free will, that we can alter the outcome. The interplay between the predetermined events and personal free will is what creates the drama of our life. Destiny determines the stage setting, and how we choose to respond to the circumstances of our life determines whether we grow, stagnate, or backslide.

Natural disasters are usually considered beyond our control. Yet even in situations that appear to be random, we are not victims of circumstance. All that occurs is happening for our spiritual growth. Our Higher self is fully aware of all that is taking place in our life. Our attitude about these events, and how we choose to react to them, will determine the eventual reality we create.

> Wildfires occur frequently in the Sierra Nevada Mountains. One dry summer a two-thousand-acre fire consumed several homes, one of which belonged to a couple who were patients of mine. Don and Carla lost practically everything. They were able to salvage a few photograph albums and important documents, but otherwise their entire dwelling was decimated. I saw them three days after the fire when Don lacerated his arm while going through the rubble. As I

was cleaning and suturing the wound, they both expressed many emotions about their tragedy. Don was very angry. Their insurance company was slow to respond, and he was furious with their insurance agent. He complained of headaches and muscle spasms in his upper back. Carla, on the other hand, was very quiet. She kept wiping away tears, her face tight with anguish. Her beautiful home had been destroyed, and from her perspective, so had her life. When they returned a week later for me to remove the stitches, Don was still enraged and Carla's depression had worsened. I referred them both for counseling and ended up prescribing medication to help them cope.

Don and Carla have never recovered completely from the effects of the fire. To this day they both exhibit signs and symptoms of post-traumatic stress disorder. The reality this couple has created by virtue of their emotional and mental reaction to the serendipity of Mother Nature has altered their entire outlook on life. They feel like victims of circumstance, imprisoned by fear and anger. Caught up in their individual worlds of self-pity, they began to pull away from each other, becoming more isolated and afraid. They remain two lonely and fearful souls, drifting and floundering, battered by external events, and lacking the anchor of faith and hope to ground them.

Warren and Fran, on the other hand, reacted differently when the following year a wildfire roared through their small community. After they were forced to evacuate when their home and most of their possessions were destroyed, fellow members of their church came to their assistance and surrounded them with loving support. Everyone rallied by cleaning up the terrible mess, donating clothing and other necessities, and providing encouragement and reassurance whenever needed. Once the initial shock wore off, Warren and Fran were able to channel their energies into getting their lives back on track, focusing mostly on the present and the future, and allowing the past to slowly recede into memory.

A month after the fire, at their annual physical exam, Warren and Fran appeared calm as we spoke about the fire. They felt sad about all that they had lost, but they did not feel devastated. They told me about a soulful conversation they had had soon after the fire. Lying in bed together, worried and a bit overwhelmed, they tried to make sense of all that had happened. Among the subjects they discussed that night was whether God had turned His back on them. Immediately the thought of all the generously offered kindness they had been receiving from friends and family came to mind. The fire, in a twist of fate, became a wonderful opportunity for many people to demonstrate love—which, after all, is really what God is all about. What began as a disaster was transformed into a truly spiritual experience that encircled a group of caring human beings in a shroud of lovingkindness. Warren and Fran found comfort knowing they were not alone. They felt the presence of their Higher Power through the warm-heartedness of others. As an aside, their lab work came back within normal limits, and I never had to treat them for any stress-related illnesses or prescribe any medication for them.

Having established that we and our Higher selves are working together to co-create our lives, how do we go about making things better for ourselves? The key to creating a reality more to our liking is through the power of our mind—our thoughts and our feelings. By making a conscious intention to change our way of looking at the world, we create a new reality for ourselves.

How can changing our thoughts alter our reality? The answer begins with an explanation of *reality*. What is real? Reality is a perception. For example, two people witness an accident. What each person sees or hears determines what he or she believes happened. Depending on where the two people were standing, their view of the accident will vary slightly. Each person thinks that what he or she perceived is absolutely what happened. In truth, they are both correct. What one person witnessed is real for him. And what the second person experienced is real for her. Yet there are small differences in their recollection of the event.

New age physics, quantum mechanics, explains how the perceiver alters the outcome of any occurrence by virtue of his or her uniqueness. Both witnesses to the accident honestly relate their versions of what happened, and indeed they are *both* accurate, even though their stories vary somewhat. So what is real? Both versions are real. The point is that *reality* is the variable. What each perceives to be true is true for them. What each think to be true is true for them.

Depending on what we perceive to be true will determine *our* truth. Your truth and my truth may vary slightly, based on the variability of what we both perceive, and yet your truth and my truth are both real. Your truth is real for you, and my truth is real for me. We are both truthful. And we are both experiencing true reality. But your reality and my reality will be slightly different.

Perception, therefore, is the key to reality. What any individual perceives to be true *is* true … for him or her. Our truth, based on our perceptions, is true for us. If our mind is convinced that what we observe is true, it is true. What we think, therefore, determines what we believe to be true. As we think, so shall we be.

If we choose to *change* what we think, with the power of our free will and the forcefulness of our intention, we will change our reality. Both our old reality and our new reality are valid—they are just different. One is real at one moment in time, and after our perception or thought changes, the next reality we experience is *also* real. Equally real. Just different. New and improved, so to speak.

The concept of co-creation is more understandable if we think of it from the perspective of energy. Energy is constantly flowing. Within each individual, energy flows in one of two directions. It can flow downward from our Higher self or ego to our mind, generating thoughts and feelings that affect the body. Or the energy can flow in the opposite direction, resulting in thoughts and feelings produced by the mind influencing our Higher self and our ego. Therefore, the energy flow chart presented previously needs to be amended.

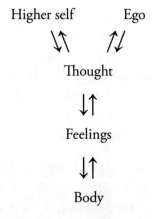

Higher self   Ego

Thought

Feelings

Body

When we make an intention to create a new reality of *our* choosing, to influence an outcome to our benefit, we reverse the flow of energy. There is a constant intuitive dialogue going on between self and Higher self. Using the power of intention, or will, we create thoughts and images that are projected *passionately* in retrograde fashion to our Higher self, to make happen what we want. The intensity of our desire to change our reality determines the degree of influence we have on our Higher self. Our Higher self is both a spiritual guide and a faithful servant. As long as what we ask for is for our best and highest good, our Higher self will gladly accommodate our new request or intention. It does so by subliminally affecting the choices our self makes.

All thoughts, conscious and unconscious, directly affect our Higher self. Powerful and emotionally charged *unconscious* thoughts affect our Higher self as much as our conscious ones. This is why negative self-talk ("I'm not good enough") undermines our efforts to succeed. The source of our negative thoughts is our ego. Our ego has a profound influence on our thoughts. The ego generates fearful or negative thoughts, just as the Higher self is the source of loving or positive thoughts. Through a feedback mechanism, the negativity of ego, working through the power of the mind, sends negative energy upward to our Higher self, undermining the outcome.

Fear is a very powerful emotion. When it appears, it dominates all other feelings. When politicians, the media, or authoritative people use fear to manipulate us, our first instinct is to react negatively—with anxiety, anger, hatred, bigotry. Therein lies the power of evil. Evil generates negative thoughts through its henchman, the ego. Our hope lies in the power of our mind, augmented by the power of our Higher self, to override the darkness with our light.

This struggle between good and evil is a constant interplay occurring at both a conscious and subconscious level. Positive and negative thoughts are both affecting the outcome of this co-creative process, influenced strongly by the intensity of the feelings behind the thoughts.

Fear-driven unconscious negative thoughts initially take precedence—it's a survival instinct to respond instantly to danger. But we are capable, through the power of our mind, of creating a less fearful reality if we so choose. Each of us is capable of transmuting negative thoughts and feelings that appear impulsively as a first reaction in any fearful situation to more positive ones. What is required to accomplish this is a conscious awareness of fear-based thoughts and feelings, and a desire to change them.

When we hear ourself either saying or thinking something negative about our self, we stop, and say or think, "Cancel, cancel." In effect, we are communicating to our Higher self our intention to change our reality—to change our perception of ourself. By doing this, we erase the impact of our ego's negativity. Ideally, we then say or think the opposite, ending with a strong message to our Higher self that we choose positive over negative, love over fear.

> I'm driving to work on Monday and notice myself thinking, *This is going to be a very stressful day.* I observe myself being negative. So I say, *Cancel, cancel.* As I begin to breathe deeply, I think, *I will be calm, I will be calm.* It worked. Another time, I'm about to give a talk to a group of medical students on a controversial subject and start to worry, *They're going to think I'm crazy or unprofessional.* As I notice the start of a knot in the pit of my stomach, I close my eyes, breathe slowly, and think, *I will to do thy will, O Lord, I will to do thy will.*

*   *   *

Another factor in creating reality is the concept called the Law of Attraction. It states that we attract to ourself that which we think and feel.

To better understand this concept, we need to look at our self again from the perspective of energy. All of us have an electromagnetic field of energy within us and around us. Electricity—energy—is either positively or negatively charged. This field contains the sum total of all forms of energy that make up a human being—physical, mental, emotional, and spiritual. Physically, our heart, brain, and nervous system generate electricity that creates an invisible grid that surrounds our body and interconnects with every cell within it. Our thoughts and feelings also have energy that is capable of influencing others and feeding back on our self—our body and our spirit. Our soul's energy also contributes positively or negatively to our total electromagnetic energy.

When the energy we produce at all four levels is combined, the summation of all positivity and negativity has a direct influence on everything we interact with and all that we create. Our energy affects energy all around us. Not only does our energy affect other people, but the power of our thoughts and words extends to inanimate objects as well. Masaru Emoto has demonstrated that pleasant things— words, pictures, music—cause water to freeze into crystals that form symmetrical and elaborate patterns when frozen while exposed to these positive or pleasing things. When water was frozen while being exposed to negative sounds and images, on the other hand, chaotic and misshaped crystals formed. The pictures of ice crystals in his book *The Hidden Messages in Water* show vividly that the energy we put out directly affects all that surrounds us. Each of us affects everyone else, and we are influenced by all that is around us as well.

Positive thinking and tranquil emotions result in an increased likelihood for creating a positive reality, whereas fearful thoughts and angry emotions attract negativity. For example, if we are angry and yell at someone, they in turn will react by also becoming angry. Smile at someone and they most likely will respond with a smile. Like attracts like.

And yet opposites attract. The paradox is that both are correct. At a physical and psychological level, opposing energies are drawn to each other. Using relationships as an example, males and females are attracted to each other to procreate. Their personalities are usually complementary, one more outgoing and one more quiet. At the spiritual level, however, like attracts like. We are drawn to people with whom we share similar beliefs and values. Misery seeks company for those who choose blame and victimization. But when we are seeking spiritual growth, however, surrounding ourselves with like-minded individuals fosters encouragement and accelerated progress.

It makes no difference whether our thoughts and feelings are directed outwardly at others, or directed internally toward ourselves; the effect on the outcome is the same. Being hard on ourselves or criticizing others *both* generate a negative electromagnetic force field. Being kind to others and gentle with ourselves adds positivity to the energy grid.

At a subliminal level, the overall energy contained within our force field manifests as attitude. Those with a "bad" attitude walk around with a chip on their shoulders, interact with others more harshly, feel anxious or depressed, and don't smile or laugh much. As our souls evolve, as we shed layers of negative thoughts about ourselves and others, we become happier. We enjoy being with people, feel hopeful about the future, and carry ourselves with a more upbeat and buoyant demeanor.

How we feel on the inside determines the attitude we project out toward others. Being negative inside translates into interacting with others negatively. When we get angry or judge someone, we are subconsciously angry at and critical of ourselves. The resulting reality we are creating, the quality of the interaction between ourselves and those around us, is therefore determined by us, by *our* thoughts and feelings. Our negativity causes others to react negatively, which affects the outcome accordingly.

Our thoughts affect our behavior. If the reality we want to create is having more friends, for example, then we should act more friendly toward others. We want friendship, so we become friendly. If we want love, we should be loving. The more we give, the more we shall receive.

If what we desire is more money, we must *behave* as someone who is wealthy. Affirmations alone will not get us what we want. We must convincingly think and *act* rich. We begin to set realistic goals for ourselves and then work hard to accomplish them. When spending money, do it in a manner that a wealthy person would. Wealthy people don't become rich by giving all their money away or spending it frivolously. By the same token, the attitude of wealthy individuals is "I'm worth it." They buy high quality (on sale if possible), tip generously, donate money to charity (as much as their budgets will reasonably allow), and not deny themselves something they really want because they feel unworthy to give to themselves.

Our thoughts and actions must be congruent when attracting what we want. We can't say one thing and then do another. If we want to attract love, and we tell people we love them, we also need to behave lovingly toward them. Likewise, if we want money, we need to be generous. If we want happiness, we need to be happy. As Mahatma Gandhi said, "Be the change you want to see in the world."

Affirmations work only when our conscious *and* unconscious intentions are aligned. We may want something, but if we don't feel worthy enough to deserve it, we undermine our efforts and negate the likelihood for success.

Penny had many years of experience working both the front office and the back office for another doctor in my community. She heard about an opening for an office manager and wanted to upgrade her work status. Because she had no previous experience as an office manager, even though she was qualified in most of the skills required for the position, she did not feel confident about landing the job. At the interview, Penny impressed the employer with her knowledge and personality, but he abruptly ended the interview after the second time she said, "Even though I've never actually been an office manager." Penny later realized that by conveying a lack of self-assurance, she had thwarted her efforts for advancement. Three months later she went for another interview, this time with a positive attitude about herself and her abilities. She got the job.

We attract to ourselves what we expect. Life is always bringing us opportunities, but if we're not expecting or anticipating them, we don't notice them. Our brain is selective in what it chooses to focus on. Many stimuli bombard our nervous system every second. To avoid being overwhelmed, our brain screens out most sensory input, so we are not consciously aware of most things occurring in our environment. Our brain will focus on things we pay attention to and disregard the rest.

When attempting to change our reality, we first have to establish a mind-set of what we expect to happen. We need to go beyond wishing and hoping. By anticipating that what we want to happen will occur, we open our awareness to that possibility. When opportunity presents itself, we will be prepared to respond and take advantage of the situation.

If we tend to be pessimistic and expect negative things to take place in our life, that's what we will notice. Even though many good things may be happening, focusing on the negative means the reality we are "creating" will be perceived as undesirable. We will dismiss all that is good in our life. On any one day, life is both good and bad—for everyone. What do we choose to focus on? It's not that we deny the pain; we simply choose not to dwell on it. An attitudinal adjustment has profound consequences.

Be careful what you wish for. Our Higher self is aware of all our thoughts and will comply with our wishes. If we desire something, but haven't considered the long-term consequences of having it, we may get it and then regret it.

Unfortunately, we don't always get what we want. There are two reasons why. The first, Divine will or prearranged agreements between our Higher self and Higher Power made before our birth, creates situations designed to give us the opportunities to learn the lessons we need to learn. We may want a million dollars, but if our Higher self realizes that financial difficulty is what we need in order to learn one of our important life lessons, fortune will elude us.

The second reason for not getting what we want has to do with our *unconscious thoughts.* We may consciously want something to happen, but will often undermine achieving our goal with negative self-talk. We may want a million dollars, but our ego feels unworthy of receiving such a wonderful gift and unconsciously manipulates us to fail — so we do or say something "stupid" that sabotages our efforts.

What happens energetically when we attempt to achieve something that we really want, but secretly have doubts about our ability to succeed at it, is the creation of a life-choice dilemma.

Our mind must choose to follow our desires or give in to fear. At this point our Higher self steps back to allow our free will to prevail. If we subvert our desires with negative thinking, we will fail in our efforts. This in turn will set us up for yet another opportunity in the future for us to face that same challenge again. Our Higher self "allows" a negative outcome to occur, patiently waiting for us to be courageous enough to finally overcome our internal fears and doubts. When we eventually convey to our Higher self, through strong effort and a positive attitude, our intention to prevail, our Higher self willingly complies with our determined efforts and works synergistically with us to resolve this karmic issue. Success, therefore, becomes a co-creative process — us and our Higher self, in harmony.

*   *   *

The power of the mind can be demonstrated by observing the *placebo effect.* A placebo is a fake pill that researchers use as a control when testing the effects of a new medicine on test subjects. Half the group gets the real medicine, and half are given a "sugar pill" or placebo. Interestingly, a significant percentage of people will experience the expected benefit even when given the placebo.

If we think something is going to help, it is more likely to do so. The more passionately we believe it, the stronger the effect. Expectations, one way or the other, strongly influence outcomes.

The power of our thoughts can also be illustrated by observing people's reactions to stressful situations. When scientists simulate a dangerous condition, people react in a similar, albeit less intense, fashion to how they do in real, perilous circumstances. If we *think* we're in danger, our body reacts as though we're in danger and responds accordingly. Adrenalin is released immediately into the blood stream from the adrenal glands, resulting in a classic fight-or-flight response.

*

The mind has the power and ability to create many things, including illness. We are capable of making ourselves sick. If we are afraid there is something wrong with us, even if nothing can be found through examination or testing, and we persist in this belief, we can cause our body to manifest the exact disease we dread. Repeatedly thinking that we have, or will have, whatever illness we are ruminating about results in the creation of a psychosomatic disease. *Psych* refers to the mind, and *soma* refers to the body.

The process begins with the ego-driven mind creating a negative thought. The thought then follows two pathways—down to the body, and up to the spirit. The mind-body connection stimulates the nervous system to produce neurochemicals that in turn alter the immune system's surveillance mechanism. The mind-spirit pathway sends a strong message to our Higher self. If it is ultimately beneficial for our soul's growth to experience this illness, constantly dwelling on the thought generates the negativity necessary to create an energetic force field conducive to the formation of disease.

So, to our list of reasons why we become ill-genetics, lifestyle, stress, spiritual growth-we can now add self-creation. The abnormal anxiety over one's health experienced by a hypochondriac, for example, creates an imaginary illness that eventually can be transformed into an actual disease state. What we fear the most we can draw to our self through this co-creative process.

> I met Howard seventeen years ago after a talk I gave to a support group for panic disorder. Among his many fears, fear of cancer was his greatest worry. Every ache and pain triggered an uncontrollable anxiety that he had cancer. Any abnormal lab result prompted the same question: "Could that be cancer?" My reassurance alone was insufficient. He required an X-ray to rule out cancer, or a referral to a specialist who would do a procedure to prove there was no cancer present. As his family doctor, I would patiently reassure him at *every* office visit that there was no cancer currently in his body. He picked right up on the word *currently,* which only fueled his cancer phobia even more. We had many discussions about his real concern—death. Howard lacked faith in any religious or spiritual philosophy. He doubted the existence of any invisible entity, scoffing and contorting his face at the mention of God or Higher Power. Nothing I said would console him. The only medication he could take without side effects was Valium. Because nothing short of a coma could stop his incessant worrying about cancer and death, I limited the prescription to the lowest dose that would allow him to be able to leave his house. He saw a psychologist on a regular basis, every one or two weeks for an hour. He and I met every two weeks for thirty minutes (although our visits often lasted forty-five minutes).

Attempts to set the appointment time more than two weeks out *always* resulted in an emergency office visit before the scheduled appointment.

Howard was basically a healthy man with good genetics. His mother was apparently as neurotic as he was, and she lived to ninety-two. Her death was a real blow to him. He felt completely abandoned, floundering without the spiritual wherewithal to make sense of her passing. He went into a deep depression. Two years after her death, his wife was institutionalized with a rare neurological disorder, further compounding his sense of isolation. He became so pessimistic that even his children could barely tolerate him.

For the last five years of his life, Howard lived alone. Every year seemed to age him by three. His obsession with cancer and death became even more pronounced. No one could stop his downward spiral. During those five years he developed diabetes, and his hypertension and irritable bowel syndrome worsened. One day I received a call from the E.R. He had passed out at his daughter's house. Part of his admit workup was a routine chest X-ray. Three masses were discovered around his heart and lungs that had not been present one year earlier. An aggressive form of lymphoma was diagnosed. Howard's cancer progressed so quickly that he was never able to return home. He died three months later. In all the years I knew Howard, he chuckled a few times at the ironies and ludicrousness of life, but I never knew him to be happy. Howard epitomized suffering.

*

Our mind has the potential to be a powerful creator. Every artistic endeavor is a reflection of human creativity. When the source of a person's creative energy is their Higher self, the outcome will be good. Once the ego and all its associated fears dominate, the result will be tainted by negativity. Human beings can create art, and human beings can create illness.

> Marletta was only twenty-eight years old when she came to see me for a lump that had recently appeared in her right breast. Although her youth made the diagnosis of cancer less likely, the hardness of the mass and the lack of tenderness made me suspicious. The mammogram showed a solid tumor. I referred her for a biopsy.
>
> Marletta returned to my office two weeks later, bringing her mother, Gail, for moral support. Marletta was stunned to hear that the biopsy revealed a malignancy. Her mother's reaction, however, went beyond shock. Gail was totally devastated. "It should have been me getting cancer, not my lovely young daughter," she said. "She has her whole life ahead of her. I wish it was me who had cancer, not her. If I could take her cancer away and give it to myself, I would." Gail's reaction was so intense that Marletta ended up consoling her mother rather than the other way around.
>
> Gail had been my patient for years, but I began seeing her more regularly after the diagnosis of Marletta's cancer to address her own symptoms of situational depression. She ruminated constantly about Marletta. At every office visit she would say at least once or twice, "I wish it was me, not her. I wish it was me."
>
> Eighteen months after Marletta's biopsy, Gail presented to my office with a lump in her right breast. Medical protocol was followed. Gail's wish came true. The biopsy was positive for cancer.
>
> To date, both mother and daughter are alive and well. Marletta got married to her fiancé and started a family. Gail

dealt with her own cancer with a matter-of-fact calmness that persists to this day.

*

Let us use the example of cancer to demonstrate how a disease becomes created. A soul will choose a body that is genetically predisposed to cancerous growths. Free will affects the habits and lifestyle choices that increase exposure to carcinogens (cigarette smoke, direct sunlight, postmenopausal hormones, and so on) that cause the cellular mitotic mutations that initiate the actual formation of the tumor. Symptoms will develop. Whether one heeds these early warning signs and seeks medical care is also within the realm of free choice. After the diagnosis is made and the stage of advancement is determined, and while going through whatever treatment is necessary, attitude plays an important part in the process. Negative thoughts and feelings impede the immune system's self-healing, whereas positive ones enhance the allopathic and/or alternative therapies being used.

Despite the best of modern science, and the most hopeful of attitudes, the cancer may relentlessly progress toward physical demise. In this situation, creating your own reality acknowledges that we have done everything within our power to achieve a cure, and if death becomes inevitable, there is an acceptance that Divine will shall prevail, and that the final lesson to be learned revolves around a peaceful transition to the next level of consciousness. Blame is released, and attachment to physical form is given up as we embrace our Higher Power. This is not seen as failure. Death is inevitable for all of us. Creating our own reality means creating our own transition. The style with which we do this is within our control. Major spiritual growth occurs during the dying process. The level of our soul's maturation will determine how we approach attitudinally our impending departure from that which is known. The inner strength of our convictions and the insights gained through life experiences will greatly influence our spiritual advancement.

*

The concept of creating our own reality is a double-edged sword. On the one hand, the power inherent in co-creation allows us to alter our own destiny and create self-healing. On the other hand, it can be used as a blaming device for self-deprecation. "I am bad. Look what I have done to myself. I have caused myself to be ill." The attitude of blame and self-chastisement is a direct reflection of low self-esteem generated by the ego during childhood.

Beth had been researching alternative treatments for cancer when she came across a book that discussed using the mind to help the body heal itself. She reasoned that her mind must have caused her cancer if indeed it could be harnessed to help cure her. She was disappointed in herself for allowing her mind to sabotage her health. Depression was evident at her next office visit with me, a significant change from her more usual upbeat attitude. Upon questioning, she revealed the head-trip she was putting herself through. Fortunately, Beth was open-minded. She could accept that her unconscious mind may have been responsible for orchestrating the lesson plan for her spiritual growth, but that consciously she did not intentionally will herself to be ill. She was able to grasp the concept that the unconscious mind works independently from the conscious mind. Beth realized that blaming herself was inappropriate and irrational. It took several weeks of soulful reflection for that knowledge to go from an intellectual idea to a heartfelt knowing. Once she was able to "forgive" herself, Beth resumed her self-healing regimen: visual imagery, an organic vegetarian diet, a daily walk along a nearby lake, prayer and meditation. Seven years after surgery, and having completed her courses of chemotherapy and radiation, Beth is alive and very well. She was able to overcome her doubts and self-recriminations. She rose to the spiritual challenge of trusting her inner guidance and its inherent wisdom. Faith in her Higher Power gave her the strength to persevere. Peace of mind replaced fear.

Because pain is necessary for all spiritual growth, and because all life experiences are occurring for our benefit, taking the negative approach of blame is counterproductive to spiritual advancement.

*

Treating illness is what I do for a living. Every day one or more of my patients is experiencing a medical condition that is, or could become, terminal. I attempt to reduce their pain and treat any side effects from their medications, surgery, chemotherapy, and so on. I closely observe their emotional reactions after diagnosing their conditions. I watch them as they go through stages of denial, anger, bargaining, and depression. Some of them eventually arrive at acceptance. At the level of acceptance they get past blame and victimization, appreciating the deeper lessons being presented, and by coming to a center, transcend suffering.

The ultimate goal in dealing with illness is not necessarily curing, but rather healing. Curing puts death off to some later date and circumstances. Although our desire is for a cure, survival being a powerful instinct, healing can occur with or without a cure. Healing is an attitude. Healing is a spiritual acceptance of *higher purpose.* It is seeing the *totality,* the big picture. We understand the soul opportunities for growth being presented—opportunities for closure with cherished people in our lives and opportunities for bravely seeing death not as an end, but as a metamorphosis. Embracing a final outcome, desired *or* undesired, requires a faith that all that happens does so for our soul's benefit.

Karma is about cause and effect. Illness is about karma. Illness befalls us all, caused by the different reasons discussed previously.

Once we become ill, a physical or emotional problem has the effect of becoming an opportunity for personal and spiritual growth. Everyone has karma, and everyone has illness. How we choose to react to illness is a reflection of who we are and where we are in our spiritual evolution. Given a situation that is beyond our control to prevent, we can use the power of our intellect to alter the outcome, or at the very least, our attitude about the end result. When we experience physical or emotional harm, creating the reality, through the power of our thoughts and feelings, that we are victims of a calamity, we suffer. Accepting that there is a purpose behind all events, the more positive approach to any difficult situation is to look for the underlying lessons or benefits. This will result in a personal attitude that allows for less resistance, less fear, less disappointment, and consequently, more serenity.

Death is a transition, not an end. There is life after life. We lose the body. We lose the ego. Our soul lives on. Born egoless, we developed this psychic armor to safeguard ourselves from life's pains. At death the ego becomes useless (as if it ever was of any benefit) and is shed. What persists after death is a manifestation of Invisible Energy. Spirit, that individual spark of Light that inhabits a physical body temporarily, returns to the peaceful wonderment of the other side. Previously shrouded in fear of the unknown, new insights gleaned from near-death experiences describe the pleasantness and bliss felt by those who experienced, and ultimately survived, death. Although dying may be painful, death is extraordinary ... certainly nothing to fear.

Chapter 4

Connecting

Holism, the interconnection of all parts as they relate to and affect each other, is a concept applicable to health and illness. The four components that make up the healing circle are physical, mental, emotional, and spiritual. Each contributes to the health, or disharmony, of the entire organism. If any one area is weak, all are affected. Like a car driving down the highway of life, if any one tire is deflated, the vehicle is forced to slow down. When all four tires are inflated, we can zip along on our journey, progressing more rapidly toward the goal of wholeness. In modern times the weakest of the four elements, the least inflated tire, is spirit. Technology has made great advances in treating physical ailments. Psychology is successfully alerting us to emotional roadblocks, teaching us how to navigate around the potholes of our existence. Recently the concept of positive thinking, creating a better life by choosing to be assertive and self-loving, has opened a big opportunity for healing negative mental attitudes. Spirituality, however, is an area many people ignore. Monetary gain is more important than ethics and principles. As a society we have lost our moral compass.

Without spirituality, life is a burden. The pains are horrible, and the suffering is unbearable. One falls prey to the victimization of punishment ... "I am bad and deserve all that happens to me." Shame and blame. Spirituality on the other hand offers hope. It provides perspective on human difficulties. There is a higher purpose to the illusion of suffering, there being a goal of soul growth toward the perfection of Source.

Religion has historically provided comfort during times of hardship. The path to salvation is offered with the guidance of a powerful church and its selected leaders. Although in many communities organized religions are thriving, the overall decline in weekly worship attendance reflects a spiritual void. A vague sense of alienation and fear permeates society. Many do not find solace in theology.

Since about 1970 there has been a shift of consciousness in our society toward the more personal. It has become acceptable to nurture one's self, to seek personal fulfillment, to be individually self-actualized. Giving to one's self, as long as no one else is being harmed, is allowable. It is viewed in the positive light of self-growth, enhancing and valued. This shift has affected us spiritually as well. Having a personal relationship with God has become desirable and permissible.

Accompanying this shift, the concept of Deity as parental, conditionally loving us as long as we are good, is changing, replaced by a Higher Power whose love is unconditional. Our motive for being good is not God's approval, but an accountability to our individual soul to do our best in achieving soul growth. There is a desire to be one with God, to emulate that which is Godly. God becomes a supreme guide, an ally, a source of comfort, safety, and love *despite* our human imperfection. A more individual one-on-one relationship between us and our Higher Power is established so as to promote individuated growth. Intercession by an intermediary church or its ministers becomes unnecessary in order to access the Kingdom of Heaven. Each of us is a child of God. The only distance between us and God is the result of obstacles imposed by the human side of the equation. All that is necessary to facilitate communication is the conscious act of quieting the mind, ignoring external distractions, and focusing on Spirit.

Connecting with Invisible Energy is always possible. At any one moment in time it merely requires an act of human will to generate that alliance. God and our Higher self are always present, always available, always willing to help. All that is necessary to receive the benefits is to plug in to this Source. If we use the analogy of electricity, God is the power station that supplies continuous current that is available at any time (unlike human power companies, God never has blackouts). Following this line of thinking, we are the electrical appliance, Higher Power is the source of the electrical energy, and Higher self is the cord that connects us to the source of energy. At our discretion, all that is required is for us to make the contact. Insert cord into socket, Higher self into Source. At the metaphysical level, we connect spirit to spirit—our spirit to God's spirit. All that is needed is our desire to connect and the effort to plug in.

If someone from a more primitive culture walked into a room filled with electrical devices, he would not know where to begin as far as accessing electrical power to run the machines. He would lack the basic knowledge and practical experience to use the wonderful tool of electricity. If someone else in the room were to plug a television into an electrical source and turn it on, the amazing sounds and colors emanating from the rectangular box would be construed as a miracle to him, awesome and unfathomable. In the realm of spirituality most of us are aboriginal. The power is there, but accessing it to our advantage eludes us. With concentration, determination, and patience, however, success is a certainty.

Where does one start? Reading or hearing about the power of Spirit from others can stimulate our interest in the miraculous possibilities of connecting with this energy, thus permitting us to become receptive to this intangible concept and stimulating our curiosity to explore it for ourselves. A major obstacle to this process is our cognitive mind. The existence of God cannot be proven. Like the unsophisticated aboriginal who cannot grasp the concept of electrical power coming from a wall socket, our logical mind has difficulty understanding the vagaries of spiritual energy. Because we lack the tools and instruments to measure Invisible Energy, we are too limited in capacity to scientifically explain Deity. Because God cannot be rationally proven, or disproven, it comes down to a matter of choice.

You can either choose to believe in a Higher Power or choose not to. Agnostics sit on the fence. For years I chose not to believe. It was illogical to me that a benevolent God could exist and "allow" all the pain and suffering I witnessed. Not believing, however, did not alleviate my personal angst as a physician observing so much illness and heartbreak. Not believing made me feel worse.

Whenever I chose to transcend my logical mind and open myself to the *possibility,* at least, that a Higher Power existed, I immediately felt better. Belief in an Intelligence and Power greater than my own was comforting. The faith to believe brought the reward of hope. Serenity was possible despite all the chaos. The scientific brain struggled with the spiritual brain. The heart said believe, but doubt was ever present.

Once the incessant chatter within my head was observed, but not identified with, the solution became crystal clear. The choice was mine. Fear felt familiar, but love brought a smile. Doubt was insidious, but faith gave me hope. I decided to *act as if.* I chose to act as if God existed although I could not prove it. If I made a leap of faith to act as if there were a Higher Power, some of my anxiety was instantly lifted.

Doubt creeps in stealthily. Although we have the best of intentions to choose a positive approach, everyday life brings us situations that make us question the veracity of our convictions. Experiencing pain, physical or emotional, our own or someone else's, can trigger the response of fear and doubt. Paying attention to one's feelings allows us to realize the presence of doubt. Fear or anxiety alerts us that we are in a quandary about our thoughts and our beliefs. The antidote to fear is love—love of self and love of Higher self. But this requires feeling worthy enough to receive this love. Lack of self-worth is a major stumbling block to self-growth. To get past this often requires a second leap of faith. Despite self-doubt, by choosing to exert free will, to actively choose positive over negative, love over fear, faith over doubt, we can accept that not only does God exist, but He loves us.

Why is this important? God may exist, but for us to receive comfort we need to feel that He cares about us. If God did not love us, He would have no motive for assisting us. Seeking solace and help from Source requires the faith that we will receive it from this benevolent Being. This, however, is unprovable. Once again we must leap over the chasm of doubt with the belief that by asking for assistance we shall receive it. What may begin as a leap of faith, after repeated verification by successful outcomes, becomes a knowing.

Connecting begins with the realization that there is more to this world than we can perceive through our five senses. In order to access insight from our Higher Power, we need to switch our mind's attention from the rational to the intuitive. The rational mind uses our five senses to gather information. It is through the elusive sixth sense that we gain entry into the intuitive mind, bringing us the inner guidance we desire.

When scientific investigators use an electroencephalogram (EEG) to measure brain wave activity, the switch from rational to intuitive is accompanied by a change in brain wave activity from predominantly beta waves to mostly alpha waves. When we are in an "alpha state" of brain activity, our mind becomes receptive to esoteric wisdom by facilitating perception by the sixth sense.

The best way to intentionally promote this switch in mental awareness is to calm our body and quiet our mind. Although intuition is always accessible, it is easier when beginning to learn how to connect with Invisible Energy to become still—sitting or lying down, closing our eyes, and taking slow, deep breaths. We breathe in to the count of four, hold it for a second, breathe out to the count of four, and hold it for a second. Slowly and deeply. If we fold our hands together while breathing, they will warm up as we become relaxed, indicating that we are in an alpha state and fully connected to Invisible Energy.

Quieting the mind is not easy. The mind creates endless chatter. Thoughts will come into our awareness. This is normal. Simply refocus on the rhythmic breathing and allow the thought to pass. The art of concentration becomes easier with practice. It takes several weeks to become comfortable with this technique. With ongoing use it no longer becomes necessary to be in an alpha state of relaxation to perceive subtle energy. Intuition eventually achieves a level of clarity that is comparable to the other five senses.

Alpha is the state of relaxation one enters during such modalities as hypnosis, self-hypnosis, biofeedback, visual imagery, and progressive muscle relaxation. Historically, humans have used religious rituals, prayer, meditation, and hallucinogenic drugs to enhance alpha perception.

Intuition is not obvious. It is subtle energy. We all have experienced it in one or more of its many manifestations. Examples include déjà vu, the intuitive memory that one has previously had a given experience; two people thinking of each other at the same time; hunches or having a gut feeling about something or someone; and the voice in our head that says we should not do something we're about to do.

There are as many paths to Truth as there are individuated souls. Your path is unique to you alone. Each person must follow his or her own course, traversing the array of lessons we humans must learn in order to achieve enlightenment. Plugging in to the power of Invisible Energy expedites personal and spiritual growth. Connecting with our Higher self empowers us to be more successful by speeding up the process. Four techniques to achieve this goal are interactive dialogue, kinesiology, dreams, and insightful flashes.

*

Interactive dialogue is simply talking to God. The following technique is one of many. If you have a method that already works for you or that you discover along the way, use what is easiest or feels right for you.

If you have never established a personal connection with your Higher Power via your Higher self, one way to do so is to ask a good question. You are ill or in a dilemma; life is challenging you; you are confused or feel all alone; you are experiencing spiritual angst; you are grieving, or suffering from pain or anxiety. You want help. You feel the need to ask for guidance.

Formulate the question. Ask a more open-ended question rather than a yes-or-no one. For example, if a loved one has recently passed over, rather than asking, "Are you in heaven?" try instead, "Where are you now?" "Should I move out?" becomes "Where should I be living?" Ask the question three times, repeating it exactly, preferably out loud. It can be done silently, but especially at first the answer comes more quickly when the question is asked aloud (whispering or mouthing the words works).

So there you are, with a calm body and quiet mind, breathing slowly and deeply with your eyes closed, hands now warm. Having asked your question three times, you then remain very still. The answer will come telepathically. Suddenly within one or two seconds, a thought appears in your mind that is your desired answer. You must go with the *first* thought that comes in. You cannot tell God, "I don't like that response; give me another one." Your mind may want to change the reply, but the correct intuitive answer will always be the first one.

Intuitive dialogue is very rapid. By the time you have completed the third repetition of the same question, the answer, through your Higher self, is already formulated. With practice, the responses need not require three repetitions, and will arrive after the second or even the first utterance. Often, especially when first experimenting with this technique, or during times of distraction or stress, there may be too much "static on the line." The connection between you and your Higher self is not clear. A question is asked, but no reply comes forth. At that point take three more deep breaths and then ask the same question three more times in succession. If you get no response within one or two seconds, a deeper state of relaxation is necessary, and three to five more minutes of relaxed, slow breathing is required to get the rational mind to move aside so as to allow the intuitive mind to come to the foreground. Once again ask the same question three times out loud. The telepathic answer will appear within one or two seconds.

It takes several weeks to establish strong lines of communication between you and Invisible Energy, so be patient. Practice daily. Five minutes twice a day would be ideal—when going to sleep, and, if your bladder allows, first thing in the morning. If you get up during the night to go to the bathroom, plug in to your Higher self as you fall back asleep. All that is necessary is to quiet the body with stillness, and with slow, deep breathing allow your window of awareness to open. Wisdom from your Higher self can enter at various places in the body, depending on the individual—top of the head, medulla (at the base of the skull where it joins the neck), third eye (between the eyebrows), heart, solar plexus (pit of the stomach), or sacrum (tailbone).

Like any skill it takes repetition. Creative, artistic, and intuitive individuals will find this method fairly easy to grasp. More logical and intellectual types may have some difficulty. Persistence will pay off. Make at least a two-week commitment to attempt daily connection. Everybody can do this. It only requires the willingness to explore the unknown, the patience to allow it to occur, and the faith to believe in possibilities.

*

Individuals tending to be pragmatic and logical will probably have better success with applied kinesiology when attempting to access Invisible Energy. Kinesiology is a tangible manifestation of Higher Intelligence. A form of muscle testing, it involves the muscular and nervous systems. In healthy situations, energy flows freely between muscles and nerves, resulting in strong muscle function. If the flow is disrupted, a switch is biologically turned off, causing muscle weakness.

Kinesiology can be demonstrated in one of two ways—a two-person technique or individual self-testing. The first requires another person to apply external downward pressure on an extended arm. If the neuromuscular connection is intact, the muscles will be strong and the arm will resist against the pressure. If the arm gives way, the neuromuscular pathway has been disrupted. The second technique of kinesiology is individual. One hand is used to exert force on the other. As reliable as the two-person method, self-testing is easy and always available. It does require a few weeks of practice to master the process to the point of self-confidence and validity. Rather than using the arm, self-testing uses the muscle strength of the fingers. (Details of the self-testing technique to follow).

The primary medical use of applied kinesiology has been for testing for allergy or sensitivity to something. Exposure to a toxic or noxious substance can be reliably evaluated on an individual basis using either the two-person or the one-person technique. With two people, the subject holds the material in question in one hand while the evaluator pushes down on the other arm. When testing on an individual basis, the potentially irritating item is touched or held before testing for strength, or by placing it in the person's lap while performing kinesiology. If the muscles are strong, there is no allergy; if they are weak, the person is testing positive for an allergy. This procedure can be used for foods, supplements, vitamins, medication (over-the-counter and prescription), or any substance you wish to test to determine if at a physical level a cross reaction exists between the individual and the specific item. In the case of negative muscle testing with a prescription from your doctor, do *not* unilaterally stop taking it. Express your concerns about the specific medication. If you are not comfortable, just say you have a bad feeling about it and request an alternative option. Be insistent if repeated multiple testing is negative.

The cause for the disturbance in energy flow resulting in muscle weakness is a biological turning off of a neuromuscular switch. Through a complex cascade of chemical and hormonal neurotransmitters, nerves and brain communicate with each other with instantaneous rapidity. Being exposed to a harmful substance triggers a physical response of a nerve ending on the skin. It is then transmitted along the nerve to the synapse. A synapse is made up of the end of one nerve and the beginning of a second nerve. Nerve one communicates by releasing a specific neurochemical that is then detected by the receptors of nerve two. The chemical sent across the synapse determines the message intended for transmittance. During kinesiology testing, synaptic communication is so fast that in one second, four nerves are involved—nerve one from hand to spine; nerve two, from spine to brain; nerve three, from brain back to spine; and nerve four, from spine back to hand. Neurological impulses generated by peripheral receptor sites on the skin influence the brain, which acts as the switchbox that weakens or strengthens the hand muscles. Ongoing neurobiochemical brain research continues to delineate further details regarding this intricate system of communication.

Kinesiology can also be used as a means to plug in to Invisible Energy when we are seeking guidance from our Higher self. The mechanical explanation previously described, involving the four nerves going to and from the brain, is applicable whether kinesiology is used for physical allergy testing or metaphysical spiritual testing. What differs is the controlling influence on the switchbox. In assessing for allergy, the information the brain uses to control the switch is chemical in nature, whereas when connecting with the Higher self, the switch is turned on and off by subtle energy.

To understand the notion that something that cannot be sensed by our sight, smell, hearing, taste, or touch can cause physical changes requires an understanding of the concept of energy. Simply, energy manifests as particles or waves transmitted through space. If the particles or waves are densely packed together, one of our five senses will be able to detect them. Subtle energy vibrates at a frequency that is beyond the capabilities of our five senses to perceive. It requires the sensitivity of the sixth sense, intuition, to comprehend. The switchbox is able to sense data received through *all six* of our senses, not just the five ordinary senses we are accustomed to.

Our current scientific technology is still too unsophisticated to measure most forms of subtle energy. One that is available now, Kerlian photography, has been able to capture light energy not discernible with the human eye. Using a Polaroid camera and film in a totally dark field, photographs detect an aura of colors surrounding such living things as plants and human beings.

My first personal experience with auras was at a gathering of psychics in February 1989. Skeptical at the outset, I was fascinated to see a photo taken of me that had brilliant balls of light all around my head and shoulders, each with splashes of red, yellow, and green. Five years later, at a different psychic fair, I had another photograph taken of my electromagnetic energy field. When the woman who took the photo came over to me afterward to interpret my picture, she simply handed it to me and said, "There is nothing I can say to you that you don't already know." Somewhat puzzled, I looked down at the photo. A band of purple surrounded me, with a band of white light around the purple. The purple extended upward through the aura of white toward the top of the photograph. "You are receiving all the answers you need. Just pay attention," she said.

From then on I began to trust the information I was gleaning in meditation. My spiritual growth expanded greatly once I set doubt aside and accepted the validity of my intuition.

How does subtle or spiritual energy cause physical effects measurable as an intact, or disrupted, neuromuscular connection, witnessed visibly as muscle strength or weakness? The answer requires a more complete understanding of our Higher self and its importance as part of the continuum of self, Higher self, and Higher Power.

The self is our individual conglomeration of genetics, physical body, thoughts, feelings, and spiritual insights. The self is our personality, our ego, how we identify ourselves. Each self is unique, and no two selves are exactly the same, like snowflakes. Before birth our soul existed as a single "drop of water" in a collective "sea of energy." It chose to separate from the totality and drop down from the fourth dimension into three-dimensional reality to facilitate focused growth. By so doing, it gave us the sense that we have inherent boundaries that separate us from all other living matter. Whereas at the cosmic level we are truly all one, here in earthschool the illusion of self becomes necessary.

Higher Power is the sum total of all that exists. It is the intelligent creator and coordinator, the source of life itself. Regardless of the name different cultures or religions may give it, Higher Power is the unity encompassing all known dualities.

Our Higher self is the part of each of us that is able to connect with Higher Power. It has the capacity to go beyond ordinary reality by plugging in to a higher consciousness. It knows why we are here and what lessons we need to learn in this lifetime. It transcends time with clarity, equally aware of that which we label past, future, and present. Our Higher self is constantly with us, vigilant to all that is around us, and always available for guidance. It is that "voice" in the back of our head telling us right from wrong, communicating telepathically with our conscious mind, bestowing wisdom upon us, assisting us through intuitive knowings.

The Higher self acts as a holistic coordinator of our organism's emotions (heart), thoughts (mind), brain activity (body), and intuitive insights (spirit).

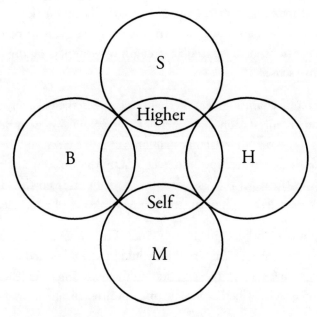

The Higher self functions as a clearinghouse for the multitude of neurological firings and chemical synaptic releases that occur constantly as the brain oversees all bodily activities. In the process, it is able to integrate input from our thoughts, feelings, and intuitions, organizing them in a synchronized fashion that becomes interactive. The Higher self sorts out and prioritizes, by degree of importance, the cause-and-effect reactions that each component has on the others:

> Heart affects mind, body, and spirit
> Mind affects heart, body, and spirit
> Body affects heart, mind, and spirit
> Spirit affects heart, mind, and body

The intuitive sixth sense is the predominant means of communication when using kinesiology to plug in to the wisdom of Higher Power. A question is asked verbally or telepathically, out loud or silently. It is transmitted to the Higher self via intuitive subtle energy. The "response" consists of the direct influence of this same energy on the switchbox that controls muscle strength during medical testing. Intuition, a human manifestation of subtle energy, is as powerful an influence on neuromuscular strength or weakness as any of the other five senses.

The exact mechanism of action that transmutes ethereal energy into physical manifestation as a chemical, hormonal, or neurological impulse is beyond the current capabilities of modern science. To date, we lack the sophistication to detect exactly the workings of subtle energy, or the exact process whereby an intuition from the Higher self can manifest as physical strength or weakness of a muscle.

All techniques for plugging in to Invisible Energy use the Higher self. The human neurological circuitry would be overwhelmed by direct contact with God energy, necessitating the buffering intervention of the Higher self. Whether via dreams, intuitive insights, interactive dialogue, or kinesiology, the Higher self becomes the intermediary between fourth-dimensional reality and human consciousness.

Yet another unknown remains, pinpointing the *location* of the Higher self. Its locus is at the juxtaposition of the physical and ethereal realms, but where specifically would that be? Having it situated just above the head between us and heaven would symbolize the spirit-body connection. Scientifically beyond human confirmation, the exact location at this point remains conjecture, requiring yet another leap of faith—a potential stumbling block for nonintuitive individuals. Explorers of the unknown have always risked failure and ridicule when venturing into areas where proof is not possible. The adventurous refuse to be stymied by the unknown or paralyzed by fear.

*

The step-by-step method of individual muscle testing is as follows:

1. Especially at first, the more clear you are the more accurate the results. Taking slow deep breaths, preferably with your eyes closed for as long as it takes to feel relaxed, clears the mind and facilitates learning. Clasp your hands together. You will know you are ready to proceed when you feel your hands warm up.
2. Position the non-dominant hand with the thumb and little (fifth) finger forming an intact circle held tightly together.
3. Place the dominant hand's thumb and index (second) finger into the circle from below in such a way that when spread apart they will attempt to break the circle formed by the other hand's thumb and fifth finger.
4. Ask yourself (actually your Higher self) a question to which the answer would be yes or no, affirmative or negative.
5. If the answer is yes, the circle remains intact. If the answer is no, the circle will be broken. Practice by saying, "Give me a

yes." Then test yourself and the circle should remain intact. Then say "Give me a no." The circle will break.

6. Once you have relaxed sufficiently and feel comfortable, you begin the self-testing process by confirming open channels of communication. You ask two questions.

   a.) Am I clear?

   b.) Am I connected?

   If the answers to both questions is yes, continue. If the answer to either or both is no, breathe deeply another three minutes and then re-ask the same two questions.

7. Now proceed to ask about any one issue or concern you have. Be as specific as possible, addressing one item at a time. For example, rather than ask, "Should I move to New York City and attend Columbia University majoring in history?", break it down into three separate questions: "Should I move to New York?", "Should I attend Columbia University?", "Should I major in history?". It is good to confirm an answer by re-asking it in different words. "Should I move to New York City?" can be changed to, "Is New York City the best place for me to move?" "Should I move to Chicago?" "Would another city be better to fulfill my destiny?" When asking about a college major, list several, one at a time, to ascertain all possibilities.

8. If you are uncertain about the answer, ask again. If the response does not feel like a strong yes or no, wait and re-test later. Life is not always a simple yes or no. Consider all options with an open mind. Your bias influences the outcome. Be as clear as possible and be open to unexpected responses. Important decisions require frequent inquiry on successive days. You can confer with your Higher self as often, and about as many items, as you want... or until your fingers get tired!

9. Counting. Kinesiology can be used to determine how many of anything you need. For example, you want to know how

many vitamin C tablets to take. Let's say the answer will be two. You ask whether you need one. *Yes.* Will you need two? *Yes.* Will you need three? *No.* You take two. You always start low and go up. If indeed you need four, you will get a positive response when asking about one, two, three and four. Five will be negative so four is correct.

10. Another method of muscle testing, called the O-ring technique, simply requires you to make two interlocking circles with the thumb and index (second) fingers of both hands. After a question is asked you attempt to pull the hands apart. If the circle remains intact the answer is yes. If the fingers pull apart the answer is no.

It's very simple once you've had some practice. Several weeks of daily muscle testing, even if for just a few minutes every day, will solidify the technique. The main obstacle to success is a lack of clarity on the part of the tester. When you are first learning, taking several slow, deep breaths before testing will facilitate accuracy. After using kinesiology for a while, there will be no need to breathe deeply or to ask if you are clear and connected. It is as if the connection is constant, requiring only our intention to telepathically connect with Invisible Energy. Fascinating!

To start with, practice the technique by asking questions you already know the answers to. That way you will be able to verify the accuracy of your testing and build up your self-confidence. Ask questions like these:

"Is my name _____?"
"Am I wearing _____?"
"Do I drive a _____?"
"Do I live in _____?"

Kinesiology can be used for guidance in many situations, both mundane and esoteric. One can ask which car to buy, food to eat, or job offer to accept. When you are making important decisions about relationships at home or at work, or if you are uncertain whether to trust someone, asking specific questions will provide valuable assistance. Regarding health, kinesiology can be used to determine which vitamins or supplements to take and how many, and whether you are allergic to a specific food or medicine. It can help you make health-related decisions such as how to treat a newly diagnosed illness. When getting conflicting advice from others about anything, using muscle testing to seek counsel from your Higher self can provide solutions.

The secret to getting the most out of kinesiology is being as specific as possible when posing questions. You may be having doubts about an intimate relationship in your life. Rather than just asking whether to continue being with this person, you may ask instead the following questions: "Is this individual my best friend?" "Can I trust this person?" "Are we spiritually harmonious?" "Will this person continue to be physically or verbally abusive to me?" "Are we sexually compatible?"

We are faced with choices many times a day. Should I do this or do that? Should I give to myself or give of myself to someone else? Depending on the choices we make, our lives will be better or worse. Decisions based on love, of self and toward others, foster spiritual growth. Kinesiology can assist us by plugging in to unconscious wisdom, helping to guide us along our journey. Remember, the knowledge gleaned through intuitive connection with your Higher self is for your best and highest good. The correct choice may be a difficult one. You may not like the answers. Be courageous.

Trusting the answers received using kinesiology will reflect your self-confidence and your faith in the intangible. With experience comes trust in the validity of the process and your personal ability to access your Higher self. Doubt undermines your efforts to connect with Invisible Energy, requiring the antidote of faith to fortify and validate your intuitive nature. Removing the doubt, even a little, reduces the static that interferes with the transmission of subtle energy from Higher self to our human consciousness.

You will find that when communicating with your Higher self, whether using muscle testing or intuitive dialogue, the results will dovetail. Psychic telepathy and kinesiology are two different ways to access the same information. Since the results will be similar, deciding which to use depends merely on personal preference and which comes most naturally to you.

*

Everyone dreams.

Dreaming is an essential part of the sleep cycle. In dreams our subconscious mind attempts to sort out disturbing feelings and thoughts experienced during the wakened state. When we dream, our eyes move around as we watch scenes unfold, causing rapid eye movements (REM) that are observable in a sleep lab. Numerous experiments demonstrate bizarre thinking and erratic or volatile behaviors when subjects are prevented from dreaming by being awakened at the onset of REM activity.

Some individuals forget the memory of a dream as soon as they become conscious. Most people remember fragments or even large portions of a dream, but with time the dreams fade from recollection. A few among us remember vividly the events we experienced while in the dream state.

As our level of consciousness changes, so does the brain-wave pattern of electricity emanating from the neurocircuitry. The awake state produces mostly beta waves. The alpha pattern is associated with meditative states that often facilitate connecting with nonphysical energy. The theta/delta pattern of brain waves found during sleep is yet another altered state of reality that is conducive to plugging in to subtle energy.

During dreams we enter subconsciousness, that part of our awareness that transcends the cognitive mind. Our spiritual essence becomes capable of connecting with Invisible Energy via our Higher self, accessing not through logical means or our ordinary senses, but rather through extraordinary means. Dreams are conduits connecting us with fourth-dimensional information.

Dream insight is elusive. Freud, Jung, and many others have spent entire careers sifting through the vagaries of the dream world. Interpretation of a dream unlocks the puzzle of hidden intelligence available to the explorer of inner dimensions. Attempting to use dreams to obtain insights can often be confusing or frustrating. Dream dictionaries that interpret possible meanings of objects or occurrences in a dream are one way to use logical thought to arrive at concealed wisdom.

Determining dream significance need not be analytical. Great awareness can be acquired by simply lying in bed in that semi-awake state as you get in touch with the stream-of-consciousness feelings or thoughts generated by the dream memory lingering as you transition from sleep to waking consciousness. Intuitively following the thread of emotions generated by the dream—fear, excitement, sadness, joy, love, hate, and so on—can be a wonderful technique for determining obscure feelings being carried around subconsciously at a deeper soul level. When you are uncertain about conflicting feelings or thoughts about the dream, asking questions using kinesiology can clarify meaning and therefore benefit your spiritual growth.

Because the memory of a dream can fade very quickly, it is often advisable to keep a journal and pen right by your bedside to jot down words, phrases, ideas, and emotions that come to mind. Write down as many details as you can recall. This is done *immediately* upon awakening, preferably while still in the limbo state before achieving fully wakened consciousness. Dream journals allow more extensive exploration of significance long after the actual memory of the dream fades. Taking one or two minutes after completing the journal entry to contemplate the nuances evoked by the dream can give valuable intuitive insight into the messages from beyond.

Dream work can be facilitated by making an intention, before falling asleep, to remember a dream. Although it may not work every time, consistently telling yourself at bedtime of your positive intention regarding dream retrieval will send a clear message to your Higher self.

A dream catcher can be a wonderful ally when attempting communication with Spirit. Many other talismans can be used as well. It is not so much the powers inherent in the spiritual object but the strength of your conviction, augmented by the authority you invest in the object. Whether you use a crystal or a religious symbol, you create the reality of a powerful facilitator by virtue of your faith and your beliefs. If you think it is powerful, it will be powerful.

Dreams vary in their vividness. Some are more memorable or significant than others. Dreams that occur after traumatic events or losses in your life offer valuable insight into spiritual lessons needing to be learned. Menses, the period of time around a woman's period, provides a spiritual crack between the worlds, a time when Cosmic Energy may be more easily ascertained. A variety of external stimuli, such as foods, substances, and medications, affect our dreams and perhaps the messages waiting to be shared.

Everyone can attempt to work with his or her dreams. Growth enhancement will be the outcome of such efforts. Although exploring the wisdom of dreams will be beneficial to any who endeavor to do so, those who possess the natural ability to remember their dreams in clear detail will feel most at ease with dream work. Anyone capable of vivid dream recall has been endowed with a marvelous gift of perception.

*

Connecting with Invisible Energy usually requires active participation on our part—quieting the body and mind, and then using either interactive dialogue or kinesiology to receive guidance. There are times, however, when information is transmitted to our conscious mind from our Higher self through no effort of our own, but rather as a sudden awareness or insight. Insightful flashes happen to us all the time. We're just not paying attention most of the time. Flashes of insight may happen during meditation or while walking silently. Even mindless activities can lend themselves to connecting with Divinity. Taking a shower, doing housework, driving, raking leaves, and other routine activities are opportune times to receive intuitive insights into problems or difficulties. We all experience that inner voice in the "back of our head" that warns us not to do something or provides a solution to a problem we are facing. It is heeding the message that is the key to successfully benefiting from bonding with Spirit in this manner.

*

Connecting with Invisible Energy can provide great insight when seeking answers to questions or solutions to problems in your life. Plugging in to the wisdom of your Higher self can also be used for spiritual healing.

Medicine is as much an art as it is a science. Western technology has developed sophisticated instruments to diagnose and treat physical maladies. Rigorous double-blind scientific protocols have produced medicines that promote healing … most of the time. Yet there are those unexplainable failures, and miraculous healings, that defy logical explanation. Some succumb quickly to a cancer, and others manifest a spontaneous remission. There are factors affecting illness and healing that are not quantifiable with modern-day equipment.

Healing is a consequence of a complex array of positive energies directed toward a specific area of disease. An integrative approach of medicines, complementary modalities, nutrition, exercise, and counseling are used in a synergistic fashion to strengthen the immune system and return the body and mind to homeostasis, a balanced state of wellness. Among the many beneficial factors that promote healing is *subtle energy*. The term *subtle* is used to mean "not detectable by scientific devices." Emanating from Source, when harnessed successfully, *healing energy* is a powerful catalyst for regaining and maintaining good health.

Our body requires specialized neurological apparatuses to interpret the waves of *nonsubtle energy* perceived by our five senses. We experience colors, sounds, smells, tastes, and tactile feelings through organs that convert the actual energy waves into concrete images of sight, hearing, and other sensations. The sixth sense is intended to make *subtle energy* understandable. Invisible Energy would overwhelm our nervous system if transmitted directly through any of our five ordinary senses. Via intuitive telepathic perception, however, the human consciousness can understand energy (information) coming from Higher Power and Higher self without harm, and indeed with very sharp clarity.

Plugging in through various techniques, all of which are effective, promotes the use of spiritual energy to manifest physical healing by using the powers of one's intellect, and intuition, to regenerate the body back to a balanced state of good health. Spiritual healing is available to everyone. No health insurance or money is required. It does require, however, faith and intention. In addition, one needs to *ask for help*.

Earthschool is a free-will zone. Invisible Energy exists, capable of facilitating amazing feats of healing, yet it is limited by the need for co-creation on the part of the person seeking healing. If our active participation in creating an improved condition of health were not essential, we would all be utopian pictures of perfect wellness. The positivity of God would automatically create a state of human well-being and would manifest spontaneous, across-the-board healing of all illness. That does not appear to be the case, however. Illness is a persistent component of earthschool—by design. It is from pain that we grow. By asking for help, an individual is acknowledging the existence and power of Higher Energy. By relinquishing partial control of one's health to an unseen Source, one is conceding the existence of a God Energy. Being consciously connected with Invisible Energy results in expansive soul growth and physical healing.

The goal of Higher Power, as I conceive of it, is not to make everything okay, but instead to be *available* for assistance if we desire it. Life provides *opportunity* for spiritual growth by virtue of the experiences we encounter and the choices we make along the way. Sickness is one of many situations that forces each of us to confront our fears and then resolve them to achieve a higher goal—in this case a return to physical or emotional well-being. Free will implies choice. Choosing to be healthier is a conscious desire to change the situation. Unless we want to change our health, it cannot happen. The co-creation of wellness requires human will, and God will, working together. How does God know we are ready to receive assistance? We must ask for help.

This process takes the form of communicating with our Higher Power, through our Higher self, requesting improved health. It is the willful *intention* of expected healing that creates the *thought* of revitalized health. Be it a goal of robustness, happiness, or serenity, establishing the resolve to achieve it will create that objective. As we think, so shall we be. We create our reality through our thoughts, so by thinking about being healthier we create a more healthy reality.

Despite our intention for wellness, disease may occur. A request for healing may seem to go unanswered. Why? Divine will always overrides personal will. Everything happens for a reason. If we need to learn a lesson, our Higher self understands the necessity for a physical or emotional illness to present us with an opportunity for a growth-enhancing experience. Realizing the influence of Divine will results in a calming acceptance of the need for pain and illness. Whereas asking for healing reflects spiritual faith, accepting the final outcome, whatever it is, demonstrates spiritual growth.

Asking for assistance can be formal or informal. Surrounding the request with rituals and/or objects of spiritual significance can be helpful toward creating an ambience conducive to healing. Talismans such as crystals, religious symbols, and pictures of holy masters or avatars invoke a climate of spirituality that aids in forming a personal connection with Higher Power. Incense, candles, and soothing music can also set the mood. Whether sitting quietly in a chair, lying on your back, or standing facing the four directions, healing will take place.

Merely stating the desire for a release from sickness is sufficient, even if it is unaccompanied by fanfare. The request can be made out loud or silently. It is the thought, be it expressed verbally or not, that creates the telepathic lines of communication. Thought can be generated randomly or with intention, unconsciously or consciously. Thoughts that are more intense, and affirmations stated more emphatically, generate a more powerful creative force. Emotion plays a prominent role in augmenting the healing process. Emotion is energy in motion. Impassioned feelings create a stronger force field. A heightened level of intensity will generate a more profound effect. Healing is best manifested when associated with positive energy, so positive emotions are preferable when asking for help. Fear, self-pity, a victim mentality, or any negative thinking is not conducive to healing. Despite any physical pains or limitations, requesting assistance with strong feelings of hope, love, and joy will neutralize any negativity with healing positivity.

Asking with an expectation of success will work better than having doubts about the outcome. Faith overcomes doubt. *Acting as if* a favorable result will occur is more likely to bring that about. Reservations or fear of failure will diminish the positive intensity of the request. Oftentimes a leap of faith is required to make healing happen—faith in God, faith in our ability to connect with God, faith in our worthiness to receive healing, and faith in the process itself.

On occasion healing occurs of its own accord, not through human will and effort, but as a result of God's grace—an unrequested blessing bequeathed out of generous love for inexplicable reasons beyond human understanding. These are true miracles. A miracle is an event that defies scientific or logical explanation. A rational or plausible reason may eventually be fathomed, so today's miracle may well become tomorrow's well-understood modality of healing. But true miracles come from beyond the physical realm— metaphysical. A gift from the Universe.

Affirmations are messages to our Higher self of intentions to be healed. Said simply, clearly, repeatedly, and with strong conviction, they result in positive changes. The desired outcome could happen quickly or take years. The object is the stating of the intention, not the timeliness of the outcome. Formulating the affirmation using positive terms works best: "I desire to be calm" versus "I don't want to be angry."

Both affirmations and asking for help derive their power from the concept of *attraction*. We bring to us that which we think. Thought is very powerful, conscious or unconscious. If the mind-set is "I can heal myself," the result will be more favorable. If I think, "This is all malarkey," it is more likely to fail. If we want it to work but secretly feel doubtful about our ability to alter our life or unworthy of spiritual healing, it is less likely to be achieved. A leap of faith is necessary to overcome the doubt so that healing can occur. The belief, indeed the knowing, of the veracity and vitality of self-healing is the prerequisite to the magic of healing. We must feel worthy enough to connect with Higher Energy so that we may receive its guidance and healing.

I am aware of several techniques used to promote spiritual healing. There is usually a series of ritual phrases used to invoke a healing connection. The specific words vary, but what makes the most important difference is our belief that healing is possible. When done with conviction, a clear message is conveyed to our Higher self of our intention for healing. Whether we use self-healing, or seek a trained or gifted healer to facilitate improved physical or emotional well-being, it is our personal determination and faith that is the key to success.

The greatest challenge for anyone desiring and requesting spiritual healing is asking for help without being attached to the outcome of receiving it—asking for help enthusiastically, but with detachment. What facilitates that balance is the intuitive knowing that we don't always get what we want ... but we always get what we need.

Chapter 5

Lessons

Everyone experiences pain. It is inherent in the human condition. It knows no boundaries—geographic or socioeconomic. Pain can be physical (acute or chronic), emotional (anxiety or sadness), or spiritual (doubts, hopelessness, or moral dilemmas). Pain may be self-induced by virtue of bad choices, or seemingly imposed upon us against our will by fate. We frequently blame others, feeling angry and victimized. We may blame ourselves, compounding further our psychological discord.

Pain is unpleasant, inconvenient, and undesirable. We go to great lengths to steer clear of it. Physically we do so by being careful to avoid injury, eating properly, getting exercise, and taking vitamins and supplements. Psychologically we avoid pain by hiding our true feelings from others or by compromising meeting our personal needs in order to shun confrontation with others. When despite our best efforts pain becomes unavoidable, we turn to healers of body, mind, and spirit to alleviate our distress. We buy medicines or self-medicate with alcohol or drugs.

Yet the pain persists. Feeling powerless generates fear. How are we to deal with our suffering and reduce our anxiety? Science, counseling, healing arts, pharmaceuticals, herbs, and so on help up to a point, but ultimately it is only through spirituality that we can make sense of our suffering.

Several philosophical and religious theories attempt to explain human angst. Punishment or retribution for personal sins is one explanation. Belief in random chaos, the lack of meaning to our existence beyond the physical activities of daily life, is another possibility. Some think God is imperfect and created a flawed world filled with torment. Many believe God is perfect, but it is we human beings who are tarnished, and that as a result of our denseness we have created grief and trouble for ourselves.

But to what purpose?

If there is no explanation for the pains we experience, but merely our human burden to endure what befalls us, we are doomed to suffer eternally. However, if you *choose* to believe there is a higher purpose to human affliction, the pain becomes more bearable. Acting *as if* there is a grand design to all this madness makes our agony more tolerable. Scientific verification is impossible. Humans are too limited in comprehension of Invisible Energy to quantify or qualify it, to prove or disprove its existence. It comes down to individual choice. Choosing a negative or neutral explanation, punishment or randomness, is less hopeful than believing in human spirit and its inherent need for growth.

What begins as a cognitive choice gradually transforms into a spiritual belief, a faith in that which is unprovable. Over time, plugging in to cosmic consciousness confirms intuitively a greater frame of reference that makes sense of our anguish, transmuting belief into knowing. What at first appears to be a giant leap of faith evolves eventually into understanding our place in the overall scheme of things. We are spiritual beings having human experiences. Our souls existed before we were born and chose to enter physical form so that we may have life situations that give us the opportunities to learn the lessons heretofore unassimilated. Each of us has different lessons to grasp, so we each have different circumstances to our lives. We choose the best life to provide the template upon which to structure our destiny.

As individuated souls we pre-view the basic framework of our lives. It is not just by happenstance that we are raised by those who raise us, in an environment that sets up a pattern of lessons intended to provide the impetus for our soul's growth. We will each live out our human lives, learn or not learn our lessons, and then die. Our bodies will be buried or burned, and our souls will return to the place where souls exist between lives so as to assess and process our life's experiences. How much our soul evolves during any one lifetime is a reflection of our spiritual maturation. Each of our lessons is dealt with separately. We grow at different rates. For one lesson we may make great progress toward enlightenment, whereas in another area we have more difficulty wrestling with the challenge. What we don't learn in this incarnation we will deal with in the next; hence the concepts of karma and reincarnation.

Which brings us back to pain. It is from pain that human beings grow. When things are going well, we enjoy ourselves and have fun. It is pain that makes us stop in our tracks, forcing us to deal with the situation being presented. Pain is like manure—they both stink and no one wants to be around them. They are both repugnant, yet ultimately they result in something good. Like the manure that brings forth beautiful flowers in the springtime, so pain provides us with the opportunities to learn the lessons we are here on this earthly plane to grasp. Pain, therefore, is essential for growth.

Just as the plant reaches for the sun*light,* our souls are drawn to our Source to evolve toward en-*light*-enment. Pain is a necessary part of the human experience for our benefit essentially, which is why God "allows" so much sorrow and hurt. How else will we grow?

There is no avoiding pain.

How we deal with life's challenges is the mark of the individual. If despite our best and most courageous efforts to alter the situation the pain remains inevitable, we can choose one of two pathways.

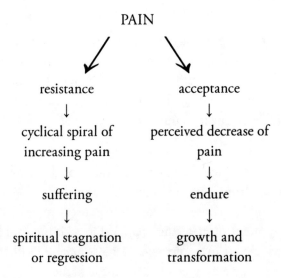

PAIN

resistance   acceptance

↓   ↓

cyclical spiral of   perceived decrease of
increasing pain   pain

↓   ↓

suffering   endure

↓   ↓

spiritual stagnation   growth and
or regression   transformation

In any given situation our free will allows us to choose how we are going to react. If we opt to avoid, deny, or resist what life is offering us, the result will be persistence, and indeed worsening, of the pain. If instead we decide to see the benefit being provided by a difficult person, situation, or feeling, appreciate the lessons, and work through them, the outcome will be positive. Acting the role of victim prevents us from seeing the opportunity being presented. We are too busy feeling sorry for ourselves to notice the underlying advantageous purpose of personal growth.

Lessons are seldom learned quickly. We are given repeated circumstances in which to face our demons, ideally each time getting more facile in coping favorably. Eventually the lesson is finally learned and the issue becomes background, allowing us to focus on yet another lesson. This process of pain, lesson, resolution, and growth is ongoing. A layer is peeled back, revealing yet another layer, another issue.

As we clear our psyche of negative emotions and thoughts, we begin to ascend in consciousness, appreciating the meaningfulness of human pain, evolving toward serenity.

Belief in a higher purpose to our tribulations permits us to see that *everything* happens for a reason. Accidents, injuries, illnesses, and family- or work-related difficulties are all designed intentionally, co-created by our self and our Higher self, to address whatever lessons we need to learn at that moment.

Our greatest challenges, and therefore our most powerful opportunities for growth, stem from our personal relationships with other human beings. Friends, coworkers, and neighbors repeatedly test our ability to choose more loving responses over fearful or angry ones. The more intimate the relationship, the more difficult the task. Those closest to us provoke the most intense feelings and are, therefore, our greatest mentors here in earthschool. Parents are our first teachers. Then as we extend outward — we connect karmically with siblings, spouse, children, and other intimates.

We are spiritually drawn to those whose traits reveal areas of necessary growth for *us*. For example, if we feel unworthy, we will repeatedly choose a significant other who abuses us physically or emotionally. Once we break the cycle, realize the dance, and choose not to perpetuate the dysfunction any longer, our lives become happier and healthier. Joy and equanimity are eventually attained.

*   *   *

Illness is usually seen as an unpleasant intrusion into our everyday routines. We judge it as "bad," viewing it as the enemy to be avoided at all costs. Many adopt a healthier lifestyle to reduce the likelihood of disease. Yet despite our best intentions, and consequent to our human frailties and our genetic makeup, ill health befalls us all.

We can choose to react to sickness with denial: "No, it's not a cold, it's just allergies"; or with fear: "I can't go to the doctor because he may tell me something I don't want to hear"; or with blame: "What a jerk I am for not taking my medicine", or "Curse my lousy genetics", or "You coughed on me and made me sick".

If instead, we approach illness without judgment, from a practical and proactive standpoint, we will be prompted to seek medical attention and to use whatever healing modalities are appropriate to restore good health.

Once we get past the initial shock of being diagnosed with a medical or psychological condition, as we embark upon a treatment plan, we can add another dimension to the healing process if we also analyze the illness from a spiritual perspective. Looking at any malady or emotional imbalance as a test in the school of hard knocks allows us to transmute pain into growth, suffering into hope, fear into love.

When looking at illness from a spiritual point of view, the outcome (healing versus persistence) is less relevant than the opportunity to learn the lessons being presented. Of course resolution of the ailment is most desired, but all too often that is not what happens. Either way there are lessons. One outcome will result in one set of lessons, and a different outcome will offer another set of lessons.

As a family physician I see a wide variety of physical and emotional problems. My practice includes males and females, and individuals in all age groups—from cradle to grave. Over the years I have seen how dramatically illness affects the lives of my patients, with each medical or psychological condition presenting its own set of lessons and opportunities for growth.

Let us now look at several common disorders, and the spiritual benefits contained within each one.

*

There are no accidents. Everything happens for a reason. All that occurs in our life is a co-creation of our subconscious mind and our Higher self. What we call accidents, events that happen beyond the control of our conscious will, are opportunities to learn the lessons ... or not ... that our soul needs for its spiritual evolution.

What we *do* have control over is how we *react* to the occurrences in our life. Our individual free will allows us to choose, and by virtue of the choices we make, influence our soul's growth.

> LuAnn was driving home from work one evening when suddenly her life was changed forever. A drunk driver crossed the median, hitting her head-on. Both drivers were going over 60 mph. Despite swerving instinctively to avoid the impending accident, destiny prevailed. LuAnn did not regain consciousness for thirty days. Life support, IV fluids, and medications were used to reduce the massive brain swelling and internal bleeding. She underwent multiple surgeries to repair ruptured organs and the two dozen broken bones of her skull, face, spine, and extremities.
>
> During the many months of hospitalization for acute care and rehabilitation, LuAnn focused on healing. She endured daily pain and agonizing physical therapy. Her sheer will and determination infused her with the strength to persevere. But emotionally and spiritually LuAnn faced the dark night of her soul.
>
> We had a heart-to-heart conversation one evening, about a month after she awakened from her coma. Her facial lacerations and fractures had healed sufficiently to permit

her to talk for a few minutes. "Why did this happen to me?" she asked. "I don't know if I'll ever walk again. There are big chunks of memory totally gone. No man will ever want to marry me now!"

Pain and depression were her constant companions. Fear was prominent. She felt devastated and hopeless. I listened to her tearful woes, nodding compassionately. I attempted to reassure her that time had a way of working things out. "But yes, LuAnn, your life will never be the same."

She returned to her former job after two years of rehab—her desk job was wheelchair adaptable. Gradually she resumed full-time work. After many years, she now walks without a cane. Her limp, however, is quite pronounced. At least she no longer requires narcotic analgesics to control her physical pain.

Although LuAnn has since moved, we remain in contact. At her last office visit we talked about her new life and her new attitude. She seemed stoic, resigned to her life as it is. She was proud of her courage and her tenacity. She had released her anger toward the drunk driver, for the most part. LuAnn had the most beautiful, albeit crooked, smile when she spoke. Her sense of humor had returned, as had her laugh. She never brought up God—her spirituality was nebulous before the accident and provided her with little comfort during her years of recuperation.

Time has allowed LuAnn a semblance of equanimity about her life situation. Anger has been replaced with acceptance. She takes pleasure in the antics of her two cats and feels less lonely living near her sister and her sister's family. She has never married.

LuAnn has learned, and continues to learn, many lessons as a result of her "unfortunate accident." Her life's journey is a difficult one. Her lessons were not of her choosing, not consciously. Circumstances, and her Higher self, have forced her to choose. Bravery won out over victimhood. Days of anger and emptiness occur less often. She can once again appreciate happiness.

*

Asthma is a condition that can be triggered by several factors. An attack can be brought on by allergy, infection, strenuous exertion, and exposure to smoke. Stress is a major causative factor as well. From a psychological perspective, constriction of the air passageways that occur with asthma can represent a blockage of emotions, a fear of expressing oneself freely.

Fred grew up in a home with a three-pack-a-day smoker. He was a good boy. Pleasing his parents had two major rewards— praise and avoidance of criticism. He grew up in a loving home, but the love was conditional. As long as he did what he was told, everything went fairly well. As a youngster he often developed croup and bronchitis when ill, but the asthma was not diagnosed until he was twenty-four years old. He met his wife-to-be in graduate school. She was not acceptable to his parents. Torn between his love for his fiancée and his love for his parents presented a seemingly insurmountable obstacle to his happiness. He wanted and needed his parents' approval, yet his love for her was irrepressible. Despite parental objection he married the love of his life. His mother's and father's disapproval persisted for years, however, resulting in continuous verbal conflict with every phone call or visit. The asthma began approximately six months after meeting his wife-to-be, and became progressively worse over the years. Medication alleviated his symptoms. It was not until a near fatal asthma attack, precipitated by watching a movie about a man who was psychologically abused by an overprotective and controlling mother, that he gained true insight into the cause of his asthma. At first he blamed living in a damp basement in grad school and growing up exposed to cigarette smoke. But his brother, despite similar genetics and childhood environmental pollution, did not have asthma. His brother, however, dealt with parental disapproval with anger, expressed outwardly, unlike Fred, who internalized his emotions. After all, the good little boy learned early on to suppress negative emotions so as to gain his parents' favor. Mother love became smother love.

Asthma is treated by avoiding allergens and by the judicious use of medication. From a psycho-spiritual perspective, asthma offers many opportunities for personal and spiritual growth. When acute bronchospasms occur for no apparent reason, looking inward may be advantageous. "What emotions am I feeling? Do I feel comfortable expressing them? What am I afraid of? Am I angry? Do I feel like I am taking charge of my own life, or am I afraid of someone's disapproval if I attempt to do so? Can I see that I am truly a beautiful child of God and worthy of love … or will I continue to buy in to the false belief that I, and my feelings, are less important than pleasing others?"

It has taken Fred many years to gain insight into his asthma. Each attack is another opportunity to deal with his feelings and his sense of self-worth. Learning to love himself has been a difficult process. Until he appreciated and accepted his *spiritual* worthiness, he could not accept that his feelings were as valid and worthy as someone else's. His humility has helped him realize that he is not *better* than anyone else, but his spirituality now allows him to realize that he is not *less* than anyone else either. We are all equal in God's eyes. Fred's self-esteem has improved nicely over the years. Rather than choosing the passivity of his youth, or aggressive anger like his brother, he has learned to be more assertive about getting his needs met. He still has a ways to go, but he is no longer intimidated by the asthma—it has now become an ally in his quest for personal power.

*

One of the most dreaded scenarios imaginable is being told by a doctor that we have cancer. Hearing the *"C"* word instantly triggers many fearful thoughts. "Will I have side effects from chemotherapy, radiation, and surgery? Will I experience pain or prolonged suffering? Will this drain me and my family of our money? How will my loved ones cope with all of this, especially if I die? Will I die?"

We go into shock as soon as we are told we have cancer. Our eyes go out of focus as these fearful thoughts and emotions flash through our mind. There are many questions, but despite reassurance, apprehension of the unknown looms prominently.

Once the initial shock of receiving the diagnosis of cancer wears off, we begin to question if the diagnosis is correct. We may seek a second opinion or further testing. Many emotions reverberate within us, from denial to anger, and possibly depression, as we face the unpleasantness of making important decisions about the various treatment options being presented. Ideally we begin to accept the situation. Many factors influence how we react emotionally and how our rational mind processes the choices we need to make, including our personality, our tendencies to be fearful or controlling, our general philosophy of life, and our spirituality.

Cancer brings us the opportunity to confront issues needing to be addressed. The style with which we handle these issues is a reflection of where we are, and how we will evolve, in our quest for personal and spiritual growth.

> Ruth received a diagnosis of breast cancer five years before I met her. She never talked about it, not with anyone. She was offered surgical excision, but she chose to shun allopathic medicine and pursued many alternative healing modalities instead. From outward appearances, Ruth was the picture of health. A healer in her own right, she focused her attention on helping others and chose not to dwell on herself.

Although we became close, I was not really her doctor. She loved me as a person, but her disdain for medical therapeutics placed an invisible wall between us. Five years after we first met, she came down with a terrible and persistent cough. It had been ten years since the breast cancer diagnosis. She allowed me to listen to her lungs. Pneumonia. Refusing antibiotics, she opted for a chest X-ray. She thought, "It's just a viral bronchitis", but she was concerned enough herself to consent to an X-ray.

It was, in fact, a large pneumonia behind one of two metastatic nodules in her right lung. That's when I first learned about the cancer ten years earlier. After reviewing the X-ray with me, Ruth became even more diligent about alternative treatments, accepting from me only oxygen during the last few months of her life.

Ruth continued working as long as she could. To her clients she explained her weight loss as a "new diet". A handful of people knew of her cancer, but it was not permissible to discuss it in her presence. Whether out of denial, not wanting others to feel sorry for her, or to continue supporting the image of a healthy sixty-year-old woman who was secretly ashamed that a health nut would get cancer, the subject of breast cancer was never discussed. Although her children knew of her initial diagnosis, they were not told of her imminent death until ten days before it happened. They confided later to me that they felt hurt that she hadn't told them sooner.

Ruth attempted to live a conscious life. For the most part, she succeeded beautifully. She sought spiritual answers to life's difficult questions. She died as she lived, a truly loving spirit. Surrounded by loved ones, she made her transition peacefully.

As I assess Ruth's situation, I see that cancer offered her the opportunity to deal with four major issues in her life: prejudice, control, denial, and fear.

Ruth grew up with the belief that home remedies were best—doctors and their medicines could kill you. Her prejudice resulted in her shunning treatment early in the course of the cancer. Surgery most likely would have cured her. She could have found a comfortable balance between allopathic and complementary healing techniques, using the best of both worlds to her advantage. She chose not to.

Control was a recurring theme in Ruth's life. She was the matriarch, ruling powerfully her family, friends, and acquaintances. She embraced new concepts, but not if they went against her mind-set of "truth." Refusing medication even for symptomatic relief from pain or shortness of breath, until she absolutely needed them, gave her a sense of control. Refusing to talk about the cancer was also her way of controlling the situation. Refusing sympathy from loved ones and close friends, another manifestation of needing to be in charge, put up barriers that deprived her of consolation, and prevented those who cared about her from giving her comfort and nurturance during her final weeks.

Denial is another prominent issue Ruth had to deal with. She realized the cancer was progressing. The enlarging cancerous mass had eventually extended to the skin and become an open and decaying wound. She began to lose weight, tire easily, and cough more often, but even with her husband, she tolerated no discussion of her condition. It took me threatening to call her children myself for her to finally contact them and admit she was dying.

How much of this was denial, and how much was fear? Ruth denied being afraid of death. Her belief was that it was not an end but a transition. She expressed joy at entering the kingdom of God. She confided to me once that one of the reasons she refused surgery and other allopathic treatments was her desire to leave this material world and all its pain and suffering so that she could merge once again with the magnificence of the Light. Ruth had to face fear throughout the course of her illness, but to outside observers her positive outlook and love for life overshadowed whatever internal fears arose.

Dealing with cancer gave Ruth an excellent opportunity to demonstrate fortitude and enduring. She never lost her faith in God and goodness.

The last thing that Louise needed in her life was cancer. As a busy and successful professional she hardly had time for a Pap smear, let alone ovarian cancer. She was not a petite woman, which made feeling a small ovarian mass difficult. By the time it was diagnosed, it had already spread to several lymph nodes, and a questionable mass was seen on an X-ray of her liver.

Surgery was the first recommendation, and she hardly hesitated. A complete hysterectomy, lymph node biopsies, and a liver biopsy confirmed the diagnosis. Chemotherapy and radiation were both advised, given the cancer's somewhat advanced stage. This shook her up a bit. She knew the toll they would take. She would have to close her office and begin a journey through hell.

Her worst fears materialized. She became exhausted, nauseated, and miserable. She was in bed or on the couch twenty-two hours a day. Louise's life shrunk down to her home and visits to the two treatment facilities. Despite losing all her hair and the color from her face, she made every effort to be upbeat. She never lost her smile, weak though it had become.

Louise has finished all phases of her radiation and chemotherapy. She has healed from her surgery. All signs of cancer have completely disappeared. She has tentatively been told she is cured and awaits that magical five-year mark of remission to be officially labeled as such. She reopened her practice, has a grateful and hopeful demeanor, and has regrown a beautiful head of hair. She is appreciative of the gift of life. Enduring cancer treatment has been her most formidable challenge. She is proud of herself for getting past her fears with her courageous and determined attitude. Fear continues to enter her thoughts every day, but it happens less often and dissipates more easily than before. Living in the present moment has been key to her focusing on happiness and gratefulness.

Louise had always had doubts about the existence of God. Cancer did not change that. But surviving cancer puts everything in a different light. She came through the illness with her body healthy again, her mind appreciative for every day, and her soul closer to the Invisible Unknown she still grapples to comprehend.

Cancer came as a shock to Louise's ordered life. *Everything* changed as a result. She had many misgivings about her ability to cope with the discomfort of chemotherapy and radiation. Her courage and determination allowed her to break through the wall of self-doubt. In the end she felt empowered by her inner strength and resilience. She felt proud that she was able to overcome her fears. What has pleased Louise the most is her flexibility. She knew she would have to give up work for a while, which for her was a great sacrifice. Her future a big unknown, she made the difficult practical decision to retire. Ultimately, however, she was rewarded by an unexpected twist in her career path.

Surviving cancer has a way of putting things in perspective. Lying in bed recuperating from the cancer therapies, she realized what her true professional calling was. She decided to follow her dream once she regained her strength (and her hair). She reopened her practice, choosing to specialize in that which was her passion, even though it was controversial among her peers. To Louise's wonderful surprise her innovative approach was very well received by her community. Indeed, she has now given several workshops for her fellow professionals, creating a reputation as the expert in her town. The sense of purpose that motivated her to enter her profession has become even greater since battling cancer. Facing the possibility of death has removed her fears of disapproval from others. Having done so, she has removed barriers to her inner joy, and enhanced her service to her community in a way she never would have anticipated she was capable of doing. Although the future of her health is still somewhat uncertain, her focus on her wonderful life in the present moment has brought her satisfaction and happiness. She lives life with a greater intensity than she has ever experienced before.

I have had several patients decide to reject surgery, chemotherapy, and radiation, choosing instead to live out their remaining time on earth without suffering all the ill effects of medical cancer treatment.

Death did not scare Ted. Being a cigarette smoker for forty-five years, he was not too surprised when he was told he had lung cancer. I never sensed fear from him about dying, only about hospitals. The mass in his lung was found on a routine chest X-ray when a blood clot in his leg brought him to the ER. Once discharged the next day he never set foot inside a hospital again. Ted had just retired. He continued his daily routines as usual. Toward the end, he insisted on staying at home with hospice helping his daughter care for him in the comfort of familiar surroundings. He assertively made his needs known and expected his wishes to be complied with. He was in charge of his own life. Both his daughter and I had no problem with the choices he made.

His health deteriorated quickly and he soon drifted into a coma. Two days later, on my recommendation, his daughter whispered in his ear that it was okay to go, that he did not have to stay for her sake. He passed within the hour.

The story about Ted's daughter whispering in his ear in order to release his soul is not uncommon. I am constantly amazed at how rapidly dying patients pass over once they receive permission, or reassurance, that leaving is okay with their loved ones. Our soul apparently needs to feel assured that our family will be okay before crossing over. I counseled one family, whose patriarch was lingering in and out of consciousness, to individually whisper in his ear their permission to go, spoken lovingly and sincerely. Afterward, the six of them left the room to get some coffee and console one another. They returned twenty minutes later to see the nurse checking his vital signs. Grandpa took his final two breaths as they entered his room.

Alex was a self-made man. Business was his game, and he was good at it. His health was failing, a consequence of his fast-paced lifestyle. Contributing to his decline in health and energy was the accidental death of his son a year earlier.

When Alex was informed that his abdominal pains were caused by cancer, and that there were already some early signs of metastasis, he elected to not take chemotherapy. He was quite matter-of-fact when making decisions. He was stoic to the end. As the cancer spread, he asked for, and received, palliative treatment from his hospice caregivers for pain, sleep, and constipation.

Before he died at home, with his wife present, we talked a few times. I was attempting to explore his philosophical beliefs about death. He was agnostic and told me he didn't want to talk about spiritual matters. In all my years of knowing

Alex, I never felt that he was happy. Business deals thrilled him, but I could not detect joy when I looked in his eyes. Despite his wealth, serenity eluded him.

You had to know Alex well to appreciate all that flowed beneath the surface. To the outer world he conveyed confidence, competence, and congeniality. In the privacy of the doctor's office, I was able to get to know the human being within. Not that he readily allowed me into his inner world. But I have my ways.

Throughout his life, Alex had many opportunities to change hurtful patterns. In his pursuit of financial success, he sacrificed close personal relationships with others. Business meetings superseded family outings. When he did interact with his wife and children, it was often with anger. Indeed, he was emotionally, physically, and sexually abusive to all of his children in varying ways. His adult children were also my patients, and I learned of their abuse by him from them. He never acknowledged it to me, and he never apologized to them.

On a few occasions Alex acknowledged feeling upset about personal problems in his family, but when encouraged to explore his feelings further, he usually changed the subject. He felt uncomfortable discussing emotional or spiritual issues, thereby limiting his chance for inner growth.

The way we deal with personal tragedy is an established pattern reflecting our emotional and spiritual development. Ideally, each of us grows throughout our life, becoming less fearful and more philosophical about the pains of earthschool. My observation of human nature, however, is that most of us are reluctant to change. Once ego-based patterns are formed, they tend to persist. Illness forces us to confront many issues that we ignore in our ordinary lives, giving us the opportunity to grow ... or not.

Sharon was not surprised when I told her she had cancer. For years she had felt in her heart that it was just a matter of time. Her grandmother and mother had both died of it. The curse lived on, even if the humans didn't.

Her medical issues throughout her life often revolved around her stomach and bowels. She was only forty-six years old, and screening colonoscopies were not covered by her insurance until age fifty. The tumor was hidden in the ascending colon, so Sharon did not become symptomatic until it had grown fairly large.

Sharon did not take the diagnosis of cancer well. Fear had always been the dominant emotion in her life. For as long as I had known her, she worried about everyone and anything. She was glued to the news channel with every national tragedy. She focused a lot of her mothering energy on worrying about her children's health.

It took several days for Sharon to process the horrible news I gave her that the biopsy was positive for cancer. At first she couldn't sleep or eat. She experienced heart palpitations and shortness of breath periodically throughout the day. We met the following week to map out a "plan of attack." Sharon decided to channel her fear into an organized assault on the enemy.

The tumor was removed without the need for a colostomy bag. She endured chemotherapy, although she had to call the oncologist's nurse three times a week about her various side-effects. For about four years after her surgery she felt like she was in pretty good health. Although Sharon knew deep inside that the cancer would come back with a vengeance, she seemed blindsided when we discovered the metastatic nodules in her liver on routine follow-up X-rays. She went into a deep depression. God had forsaken her, and she was doomed to die.

Sharon was hospitalized many times over the next ten months. She opted for any new anti-cancer drug her oncologist suggested, each one failing to halt the progression of the disease. As she lay in her bed, wasting away to skin and bones, depleted of all but a glimmer of life force energy, I offered her the option of going home with hospice assistance. Fearful to the end, she began to hyperventilate at the thought of not being surrounded by the comfort of the nurses and hospital technology. Her husband and children were by her bedside for hours every day, but they were asleep at home when she eventually passed at 3:00 a.m.

My attempts to discuss the process of transition were met with anger. Sharon felt I was giving up on her, proclaiming her death sentence. She considered religion to be foolish nonsense, and my stories about near-death experiences and the afterlife were unprofessional. She could not be consoled. She died as she lived…afraid.

Emotionally, Sharon was doomed from the start. Not only was fear prominent in her life, but she had no insight into its stranglehold on her heart and mind. Rather than seize the opportunity to confront her fear, at least somewhat, she chose the security of the familiar and remained stuck in fear mentality. Had she been more open-minded to new possibilities, she might have made inroads into grappling with her most influential nemesis … fear.

Fear is painful. It dominates the list of negative emotions. As long as we choose to identify with, and indulge in, whatever is scaring us, the outcome will be fearful—full of fear. *Every time.* If fear is our constant companion, the reality we are creating by our negative thoughts will *always* be frightening.

Transmuting fear into proactively choosing a healthier lifestyle, getting appropriate lab tests and X-rays to detect cancer early, and attempting to resist the negativity of fearfulness if cancer should be diagnosed, is a much more life-affirming alternative. The choice is ours. Overcoming fear is very difficult, but it can be done. Too bad Sharon couldn't.

> Howard was the salt of the earth. Married with two sons, he worked hard his whole life. The family attended church regularly, lived a comfortable middle-class lifestyle, and were considered good neighbors and reliable friends.

> Enjoying retirement and his grandchildren, receiving the diagnosis of prostate cancer was not welcome news. However, Howard took life as it came. Surgery ruined his sex life, but he and his wife came to accept it. Over a period of twelve years he also required radiation to his pelvis and numerous injections of hormone chemotherapy. His attitude throughout it all was matter-of-fact. Cancer was part of his life. And Howard felt he was blessed with a good life.

> We developed a close doctor-patient relationship over the years, so it felt appropriate to make occasional house calls as he approached the end of his life. I would drop by his house on my way home after office hours. Once we finished dealing with the various medical issues, our conversation turned to other matters. He had a few dreams about his mother. She was standing in a meadow of flowers beckoning him with a gentle smile. As he lay in the hospital bed that hospice had installed temporarily in the living room, his mind shifted back and forth between his suburban home and "somewhere else." He described a wonderful peacefulness as he floated into an altered consciousness. At first he thought he was hallucinating from the pain medication, and to some degree he was correct. The narcotics allowed him to

disassociate from ordinary reality sufficiently that he began to have recurring experiences that seemed otherworldly. He took great comfort from these "visits", especially after I reassured him he was not crazy. He was preparing to make the transition, and invisible entities were coming to help him cross over. His face appeared serene and blissful as he described his "dreams."

One cold winter night, as I was preparing to leave the office for home, I received a page from the hospice caregiver that Howard's breathing had become labored and he had become unconscious. I remember to this day all of us—his wife, both sons, the hospice volunteer, and me—lying or sitting on the bed with him, silently witnessing his final breaths, touching his physical body as his soul ascended. We all cried with both sadness and joy. If death can be good, Howard had a good death.

Suffering is the result of human resistance to our unfolding life. Courage is required to motivate us to do everything possible to seek a positive outcome in any predicament. But having done our best to control the situation, serenity can be achieved only through acceptance.

For all of us, indeed for everything, life is impermanent. Everything and everyone. It is the way of things. If we can accept this as is, unchangeable by our will or desire, we will reduce the influence fear has in our life.

Seventeen years ago, soon after her husband of forty-two years passed away, Judith became my patient. Two years later she found a lump in her left breast. At surgical biopsy it was diagnosed as malignant, so a mastectomy was performed. She caught it early, her lymph nodes were negative, and there was no chemotherapy or radiation. Still grieving (for her husband, and now her left breast) she had no desire for reconstructive plastic surgery, choosing instead a prosthetic bra.

For many years, seeing herself naked in the mirror reminded Judith that she could die of this disease. Fear became a frequent companion. She began avoiding glances in the mirror. She was obsessed with thoughts of recurrence or metastasis. She requested frequent exams, blood tests, and X-rays, seeking reassurance she was cancer-free. Judith read voraciously, becoming quite an expert about breast cancer. She attended, and then became one of the leaders, of a local support group. As she gained more knowledge, fear was replaced by facts. Helping others also helped her cope with her own personal fears. Volunteering to assist other women enduring breast cancer became an extremely rewarding endeavor. Fear no longer hovered around her psyche. Judith was a survivor of cancer.

Spiritual faith and a positive attitude are two excellent ways to dispel fear. So is service to others. Focusing our attention away from ourselves and instead endeavoring to be of assistance to others gives us the opportunity to transmute fear into love. Helping another attracts Light to all involved in the experience. Both the receiver and the giver benefit. Darkness cannot exist where there is Light.

Judith had no one to nurture after her husband died. Her kids had grown and become self-sufficient. Nurturing other women with breast cancer was very gratifying for her. Giving to others enhanced the compassion within her. In some mysterious way, being of service set in motion a cascade of positivity that elevated matters to a higher level.

By helping others release fear and other negative emotions, Judith observed a letting-go of negativity within herself. She became more lighthearted, heard herself laughing with her clients more often, and observed that she was less controlling and more forgiving when interacting with her sons and daughters-in-law. She confessed to me one day that she even felt less resentful toward her dead husband. This was very therapeutic, since holding on to old resentments has been implicated as a causative factor in suppressing immune system strength, and therefore predisposing an individual genetically prone to cancer to develop it. By releasing resentment, Judith reduced her chances of having the cancer recur.

*

Arthritis and other chronic joint and muscle inflammations can often become quite debilitating and painful. Enduring this every day can be overwhelming. Pain drains us of vital energy. It draws the focus of our attention away from the outer world and more toward our inner suffering. Seeking relief from the pain may lead to dependency on narcotics. Confronting chronic pain offers us many challenges and opportunities for growth.

> Carolyn has been my patient for many years. Over time her arthritis has progressed from annoying discomfort in her low back, hips, and knees to the point where she now requires a motorized wheelchair to get around. Early in the course of her condition, I prescribed daily walking to keep her joints limber and to help her lose weight. Since movement caused pain, she quickly became discouraged. Inactivity contributed to her weight gain, as did her consumption of comfort foods to help her cope with the pain. As her arthritis worsened, she became more bitter. She often got angry with her husband and coworkers, and complained frequently about all the "jerks in the world." Her increasingly inflexible body resulted in her becoming more rigid in her thinking as well. Her way was the correct way. She became

intolerant of other viewpoints, whether it was about raising children, projects at work, or religion.

Over a twenty-year period, Carolyn's pain has necessitated gradually increasing her doses of analgesics. Her escalating use of narcotics caused slurring of her speech and mental confusion. One day she unintentionally took too much medication, resulting in a hospital admission for a near respiratory arrest. A night in the ICU was her wake-up call. Although still on strong pain medications, she has learned to coexist with her pain and to modify her activities to avoid aggravating the inflammation. At first, using a walker was admitting defeat. After she lost her balance one day, fell, and fractured her left hip, she came to the unpleasant realization that pride was not worth misery. Today, she actually has fun scooting around the grocery store and willingly accepts help from others. She is less rigid in her thinking, especially about religion.

The severity of her pain made her question her beliefs. She became very angry at God and stopped going to church for several years. Carolyn has since made peace with her Higher Power. Accepting her lot in life has allowed her to release much of her anger. She now attends a nondenominational church and organized a support group that assists fellow parishioners with acute and chronic illness who need help coping with daily routines or who simply need a sympathetic ear. God is once again very present in her life ... despite the pain. She stopped feeling sorry for herself and began to focus on small daily accomplishments. Helping others changed depression and hopelessness into an opportunity to serve fellow sufferers. What began as discouragement and fear turned into faith that everything happens for a reason. She now realizes that her terrible chronic pain has resulted in a closer relationship with other people and her own inner divinity. Carolyn is now able to endure the pain with less resentment. For the most part, she has become more gentle, her scowls now replaced with smiles.

*

Acute back and joint injuries challenge us in ways that are different from chronic pain, presenting us with a distinct set of other potential lessons to learn.

Stan was excited to take his family on their dream vacation to Hawaii. Working long hours in the office prevented him from working out regularly, but he still felt youthful for a thirty-eight-year-old father of three. Excited to finally play in the ocean after hours of traveling, the family rushed to the beach to frolic and swim. Watching his kids body-surf and glide on their boogie boards looked like so much fun that Stan decided to join in the merriment. Although a few strong waves slammed him into the beach, he ignored the twinges in his back. It took one slip off the boogie board, however, to put him over the edge.

Writhing in pain, his concerned family brought him to the ER. X-rays showed no fracture, but the injury put him out of commission for a few days. Despite his initial disappointment and repeated self-recriminations over being out of shape, Stan decided to "chill." Analgesics and muscle relaxants took the edge off the pain. Lounging in the shade for a couple of days allowed him to heal sufficiently enough to resume playing with his family in the ocean, albeit more gently and carefully. An incident that could have ruined the vacation became an excellent opportunity for self-awareness. Stan decided to bring the aloha spirit home with him. He left work earlier than he had before, joined a gym, and made a conscious choice to relax more and enjoy his many blessings. It was a life-altering vacation.

Acute injuries teach us to slow down, to stretch gently before and again after exercising, and to work out in accordance with our age and our level of strength and conditioning.

*

Medical clinicians have begun using a new term to describe individuals who are likely to succumb to a cardiovascular death: metabolic syndrome. There are four components to this diagnosis: hypertension, diabetes, hyperlipidemia, and obesity. Each of these conditions leads to heart disease by itself. The effect on the heart and blood vessels is additive. Anyone with all four is at greatest risk. If the person smokes cigarettes and has COPD (emphysema), it further increases the risk.

> Hal towers over me as he stands to greet me. A bit wobbly with a "bum leg" and a new cane, he's in my office to review recent lab work. Friendly as always, he speaks in short five-word sentences with deep breaths between them, the exertion of standing and talking simultaneously having its impact.

> He is explaining to me that his blood pressure is up because of stress. He is upset that his job now requires him to walk more. At six foot three, 330 pounds, overweight, limping, and wheezing, this was going to be a challenge. He couldn't afford to quit his job, and he wouldn't admit how difficult it had become to get around for fear of being laid off.

> Hal's lab test showed his diabetes was not being well controlled, and his cholesterol and triglycerides were both elevated, despite recent increases in his medication. On examination, his heart rate was rapid and his lungs showed diminished breath sounds. Our conversation then focused

on how he was doing with the habits and lifestyle changes we had discussed previously. Again he revealed his plan to cut back on calories. "But you know what a great cook the wife is," he said. "And I'm only smoking half a pack a day lately." Of course his back and knee prevented any exercise.

I listened to his reasons for not changing, all the while realizing that Hal was depressed about his declining health. The creature comforts that had caused his problems in the first place became even more desirable now. Beneath his extroverted demeanor, Hal appeared resigned, and unmotivated to change.

The coroner called me the following week. Hal's wife had found him on the toilet, leaning against the wall. He had been ill for three days with an intestinal virus. Vomiting and diarrhea had depleted his body of potassium. His weakened heart could not tolerate the sudden electrolyte imbalance. He had died of a cardiac arrhythmia while going to the bathroom.

Hal's diet had consisted of sweet rolls and coffee for breakfast, fast-food lunches with fries and soda, and a big supper of meat, starch, and a serving of vegetable. He snacked while watching TV, going to bed every night with a full stomach. Salt added flavor, coffee and cola got him through the day, and life was not worth living without dessert. After working all day and doing his household chores, he was happy to relax in his favorite chair. He had a few beers in the evenings and a six-pack while watching sports on weekends.

Like all of us, Hal established patterns of behavior that made him comfortable and happy. The effects on his health were gradual. By the time he reached middle age, he realized he needed to be more moderate about calories, caffeine, cigarettes, and alcohol. He even joined a gym for a year. He knew what he should do, promising his wife (and doctor) he would change, but secretly feeling inside that life was tough enough and he deserved to give to himself. He was tired of people telling him what to do.

Guilt would periodically motivate him to eat more healthfully and exercise for a few weeks. But it was easier and more satisfying to go back to those things that gave him comfort. He ignored early warning signs that his health was deteriorating. He would deal with the consequences later, he thought. When he realized how bad things had gotten, he became overwhelmed and discouraged. Low-grade depression set in, only adding to his inertia. Finally, subconsciously, he just gave up. It took ten years for his body to die, his spirit having already relinquished the will to live.

*

The two parts of the body with the most number of receptor sites for emotionally mediated hormones and neurotransmitters are the brain and the gastrointestinal tract. When our feelings trigger a release of neurochemicals, our stomach and intestines are quick to respond. It's amazing how readily our mind can ignore how bad we may feel emotionally, but the body never lies. We may try to fool ourselves that everything is okay, when in reality, inside we are tied up in knots worrying about this or that.

> I remember the terror in Mark's eyes when we first met in the emergency room. Severe abdominal pain followed by a bloody bowel movement scared him enough that he could no longer ignore his body's previous attempts to alert him about his anxiety. Antacids had been his bedside companions for many years, and his three bowel movements every morning had become so routine that he saw it as normal. But recent marital issues had intensified Mark's emotions to the point that his body's distress call had to be dealt with immediately.

The hospital workup followed by outpatient testing confirmed the diagnosis of peptic ulcer disease and irritable bowel syndrome. Both his upper and lower gastrointestinal tract were involved. It took ruling out anything exotic by the GI specialist, and numerous discussions with me about the mind-body connection, for him to get past his intellect and appreciate how his body was attempting to communicate with him.

Mark is a sensitive sort of guy. He takes life seriously and feels things deeply. Whether it's worrying about the world situation or the jerk his daughter married, his gut lets him know every time how upset he is. Even with medication he can feel the acid twinges in his stomach, soon followed by the cramping lower down, whenever his daughter calls up crying.

Overall, Mark's condition has improved dramatically in recent years. Medicine has reduced the severity and frequency of his abdominal symptoms. He started walking around his neighborhood five days a week with his wife after work, before they had dinner. It gave them a half hour to talk things over, including issues between them. Their relationship has never been stronger. He began to read several books about managing stress. He was also drawn to two authors whose philosophical approach to coping with stress launched him on a spiritual journey that remains ongoing. Mark has come a long way since I first met him years earlier. It is gratifying to see how he has transformed his pain and fear into growth and confidence. Life does not intimidate Mark like it used to.

Those with a sensitive GI tract are both cursed and blessed. Abdominal pain is an uncomfortable inconvenience for anyone trying to get through their hectic daily routine. As a barometer of our feelings, the gut can be a valuable tool to warn us that all is not well in our life. The problem with acknowledging that is that once an issue is identified as a stress inducer, we now have to address it. And that's usually a lot of work, requiring emotional risks and stirring up all those feelings inside. For those consciously attempting to follow a spiritual path, ignorance is not bliss. Issues impeding our personal and spiritual growth require our full attention. Since life is a series of challenges and lessons, stress is always an issue for all of us. Each individual needs to learn their personal target organ that breaks down when dealing with problems. Rather than reacting to symptoms with fear, using our pain to gain insight and self-improvement makes illness an opportunity for growth.

*

Fibromyalgia and chronic fatigue immune dysfunction syndrome (CFIDS) often have devastating effects on people's lives. The effects are not lethal and have no obvious outward signs, so sufferers of these two illnesses have difficulty explaining to others how bad they feel. Preceding the onset of symptoms is usually a traumatic event, physical or psychological. The extreme stress of that situation paralyzes the immune system. With the defense system of the body weakened, the stage is set for the presumably viral, auto-immune post-traumatic process to begin, resulting in extreme fatigue, muscle pains, cognitive dysfunctions, depression, and other debilitating symptoms. Once the process begins, the effects appear to linger indefinitely. Symptoms tend to worsen during stressful times, and improve with self-nurturing.

> Betty always knew that her adopted daughter would ask about her biological parents. She even anticipated her child's desire to meet them someday. At some deep emotional level it worried her, however, perhaps a premonition of the intensity of that future event. Adolescent breaking away is always a challenging time for both parents and child. Betty had the

added pressure of hearing, "I'm going to leave you and live with my *real* mother!" Which she did. Betty was devastated, afraid her daughter would abandon her forever.

Approximately six months after the mother-daughter cleavage, Betty became ill. Symptoms progressed, and she eventually received a diagnosis of reactivated or chronic Epstein-Barr Virus (a chronic fatigue syndrome caused by the mononucleosis virus). A once dynamic woman with lots of energy and the creative flair to channel it into many activities and projects, Betty was now reduced to an immobile lump of protoplasm. She slept or rested sixteen hours a day, and still was exhausted. As her energy was drained, so was her joie de vie. Her whole life shrunk down to her home, what few chores she could handle, and the paralyzing depression that enveloped her.

Of note, her daughter moved back to town, and after several years mother and daughter resumed the very close relationship they had shared beforehand. They are now best friends once again. But the sequelae from the hit Betty's immune system took persisted. What she noticed was that any stressful situation had profound effects on her health, precipitating a three or four week flare-up of the condition. She also observed that when she took good care of herself, her symptoms improved nicely and she could function better.

Betty realized that giving to herself, by listening to her body and resting when tired, prevented a flare-up of the illness. Exercising improved her sense of well-being and energized her, as long as she didn't overdo it. She ate more healthfully and made a concerted effort to have more fun. As she became more grateful for the times when her health was good, she noticed that she became more appreciative for *all* of her many blessings. Love became more prominent in her life, overshadowing feelings of fear, resulting in more joy and inner peace.

Betty experiences mild symptoms when she is tired, and she accepts that her health will never be as vibrant as it once was. Upon questioning, she tells me she's never been happier.

Abigail was alive and doing well. Married, healthy, in her prime, she was enjoying her very good life. One day at work she was robbed at gunpoint. At that moment in time she thought she was going to die. The nightmares started immediately. Any man she saw who resembled the bank robber elicited sheer panic. Driving to work each day became more and more difficult. She received counseling and medication to help reduce her anxiety and insomnia.

Within a month of being robbed Abigail began to develop classic symptoms of CFIDS. By six months she was frequently bedridden and on medical leave of absence. Two years later, fibromyalgia attacked with a vengeance, further devastating her life with severe muscular pain throughout her body.

It is now fifteen years later and Abigail still experiences extreme fatigue and daily pain so intense she requires narcotic medication. Unable to exercise to reduce stress and depression, she relies on medication to control her mood. She is basically housebound. Her once vivacious life and personality has been transformed into an empty existence of pain and suffering. She has forgotten how to laugh.

Coping with the life-altering effects of chronic fatigue syndrome and fibromyalgia is a very difficult challenge. The stress of needing to change all daily routines to accommodate for the fatigue and pain is compounded by having others not understand how badly they feel because they look so "normal." They and others begin to question their sanity or want to label themselves as depressed. Which they are— but not as the *cause* of the illness, but as the *result* of it. Enduring the pain and the cognitive and emotional consequences of these conditions is a major life lesson. Flexibility is required to adapt to the necessary changes in lifestyle and work disability. Most people have difficulty accepting the need to slow down and take on fewer responsibilities. Because of the financial impact on their life, there is also the lesson of giving up attachment to money. Even more difficult is giving up resistance, and accepting the reality of how their life has been dramatically and irreversibly altered as a result of these illnesses.

Betty and Susan demonstrate that stress is not so much the result of what happens in our life, but how we *react* to what happens in our life. Life is always throwing us curve balls. Stuff happens. We can feel like a victim, or we can, once we have begun to accept and adjust to the required alterations in our life, continue to live out and even enjoy our new life as it is ... not our idealized vision of how it should have been. It comes down to making a choice: cope or give up. Those who decide on the more positive approach are happier and have milder symptoms. Those who spiral down the rabbit hole are devastated.

*

Surviving a stroke may not seem like a blessing to anyone challenged by the rehabilitation required afterward. Months of therapy is usually needed to recover from the neurological damage incurred by the blood clot or bleeding in the brain. Healing after a stroke presents many lessons as the person deals with the residual physical and cognitive defects that must be addressed.

Hazel always took pride in her ability to be self-sufficient. A widow for ten years, she had made a life for herself that allowed her the freedom to make her own decisions. Her health was

123

good, her car gave her mobility, money was adequate, and family was nearby. It was a shock when she awoke from a nap one day and stumbled as she tried to walk. Her right arm and her right leg had no strength. When she called her daughter, the words came out all garbled. Hazel came to the unpleasant realization that she was having a stroke.

It took only a day to confirm the diagnosis. Rehab took a lot longer. Speech and physical therapy challenged her to persevere as she relearned old tasks and regained her ability to communicate effectively. By the time she returned home, guardrails and other safety measures had been installed. She had her medical-emergency necklace in case of an accident or crisis. Her home was on one story, and with a walker Hazel was able to maneuver sufficiently to give her the confidence to continue to live independently.

Within six months she was driving again and was no longer dependent on her grandson to help her do her errands. It wasn't easy to accept help from others at first, but necessity gave her no other option as she worked diligently to regain her independence. As she looked back at her recuperation, she felt a sense of accomplishment at all she had achieved.

About five year later, a misstep off a curb resulted in a fractured hip. Now with both legs not functioning well, Hazel had to face the difficult decision to not live alone anymore. I expected more of a fight from her. Instead, she stoically accepted the situation and adapted well to her new apartment in a senior assisted-living facility. To this day she always manages a cheerful demeanor, even though deep inside she misses her own cooking and somewhat resents having to be on someone else's schedule. It was not easy getting used to so many people around her, but she enjoys retreating into the privacy of her room and all the personal touches that give her comfort.

How individuals handle unexpected difficulties in their lives is a reflection of their personalities and their spiritual evolution. Without judgment, it is interesting to observe how differently each person copes with change. Having the humility to accept help, and the flexibility to accommodate for unforeseen circumstances, allows one to navigate the uncertainties of life. Surviving a stroke presents many opportunities to learn patience, to learn to endure, to be less self-critical, and to be willing to laugh at the annoying frustrations that punctuate our daily routines. Attitude makes all the difference.

*

If we live long enough, we will experience the cognitive decline and memory loss that results in dementia and Alzheimer's. Maturing into our senior years presents an array of new situations that challenge us to grow ... or not. Oftentimes the extended family is drawn in, further expanding the many opportunities for introspection and growth.

> Henry has many stories to tell. And he does so, repeatedly, to anyone who will listen. He does what you ask of him, usually, and with a cooperative attitude, usually. His memory has been failing gradually over a period of twelve years. Until recently, Henry drove himself to his office visits, but now family members are taking turns bringing him. Retired and usually cheerful, Henry enjoys puttering around the house and garden. The family and daily routines give structure to his life. He used to love walking around the neighborhood and chatting with a few folks. After the third time his wife had to go out to retrieve him, however, that was curtailed. He objected to being restrained from leaving the front yard, but his wife was patient and usually able to distract him. For the

last year Henry has been on medication to control occasional outbursts of anger. Sometimes he would raise his fists, or push his wife aside, or pace the floor mumbling obscenities during the night. Despite frequent discussions about placement in a locked facility, the family continues to want Pop around them for as long as possible. By helping Mom, who is seventy-eight years old herself, the children and grandchildren cooperate to keep the family intact. For all of Henry's inner confusion, his life is good and he seems quite contented.

Paul, on the other hand, has not fared as well. Married with two children who both live out of town, his decline into the depths of Alzheimer's was more rapid, punctuated with violent eruptions that frightened his wife. Still working herself, accidents and situations arose that necessitated his admission to a locked-down unit in a town twenty miles away (all local facilities had a limited number of beds and were full). His wife now visits him on Saturdays, but he no longer recognizes her. The skilled nursing facility takes pretty good care of him, but his wife feels guilty and depressed about their lot in life. She doesn't know what she would do without the comfort and fellowship of her friends at church. And Paul, well, he's in his own world, and one can only guess what that is like.

The cognitive changes that occur with aging vary with each individual. Genetics and lifestyle strongly influence the age of onset and the degree of severity. Those who desire to postpone or slow down this process will intentionally stay as physically and mentally active as they can. Physical activity pumps blood into all the small arteries throughout the body and brain, oxygenating each cell and bringing vital nutrition. Mental stimulation improves memory by repeatedly activating nerve synapses in the areas of the brain involved with memory. Use it, or you'll lose it.

Being alone too much reduces external stimuli, so the mind is not challenged and slowly deteriorates. Avoiding isolation benefits memory and prevents loneliness.

Facing declining physical and mental health brings the issue of our personal mortality to our awareness. Although most people refrain from thinking about dying, noticing memory problems in ourselves forces us to confront the myriad of fears and expectations associated with the end of life.

Not being able to remember things is a helpless feeling. The frustration of memory loss can lead to hopelessness and depression. The style with which we deal with the entire process of aging is influenced by where we are spiritually. If we can visualize a big picture that places death in an understandable frame of reference—transition of our soul to another consciousness rather than termination—we can accept the inevitable with less worry and suffering. It also allows us to accept help graciously from others when we need it.

In my experience, those individuals who addressed the many losses associated with aging *before* it actually began, by talking with others or reading about and contemplating spiritual concepts, were less apprehensive when they observed the aging process begin in themselves. Spirituality is not something we can turn on like a light switch just as we're about to cross to the other side. The sooner we begin to contemplate "what it's all about," the less fearful aging will be for us.

*

Aging represents decline. Experiencing the downhill side of the curve entails coping with loss. As we get older, the physical body naturally wears out. We are not as strong, and we tire more easily. Chronic degenerative illnesses develop, requiring us to spend more time caring for our health. We see ourselves gradually lose control over bodily functions. Memory becomes an issue. Aging forces us to endure the deterioration of our body and our mind.

Our ability to maintain our independence is threatened as we get older. Financial concerns are a worry for many senior citizens. Observing the numerous losses that happen as we age is depressing. Fear only intensifies our emotional reaction to the aging process even more. We become afraid thinking about all the changes going on, as well as fear of the eventual final outcome.

Every stage of our life offers us different challenges and opportunities. Some of the most difficult ones present themselves toward the end of our mortal lives. Can we accept the changes occurring beyond our control? Can we adapt to the changing circumstances of our life as necessity determines? Can we resist the impulse to be afraid of all the changes, present and future? Can we detach from the physical and refocus our attention more on the spiritual? And what will death be like?

If there is ever a time when the serenity prayer is applicable, it is at this stage of a person's life. First, do everything possible to change whatever you can change. But once you realize that there is nothing more you can do to alter the outcome, ask for the serenity to accept what you cannot change.

As a family physician, I often have several generations within one family as my patients. I maintain a pivotal position between an aging parent and the adult children concerned about the health and safety of their loved one.

> Wilma is eighty-five years old, a widow for three years now, and still living in the three-bedroom house she and her husband have lived in for years. She continues to drive, even though her skills have been deteriorating rapidly in the last year. Her failing memory has more than once caused her to get lost trying to navigate once familiar routes around town.

She has fallen twice, but nothing serious has happened yet.

The biggest concern that Wilma's children have expressed to me is for her safety. They would like her to sell the house and move into a senior retirement complex. There would be caretakers to assist her, she would no longer be isolated from others, and there would always be someone present in case of emergency.

Wilma would have nothing to do with this scheme her children concocted! She is an independent woman, finally on her own for the first time in her life, and she's not about to go into "a home" any sooner than she has to. She covets her independence. Despite two small fender benders, she will not stop driving. It symbolizes her freedom. When the children asked me to take away her driver's license, I realized I needed to be an advocate for my patient. I told Wilma's children that she was mentally competent to make her own decisions in life, even if they weren't always practical. Wilma still lives on her own, and is managing just fine for now.

It's going to take a bad fall, illness, or car accident before Wilma will concede to assisted living. Until then, her children have wisely backed away from trying to get her to move. They have chosen to not go with fear, but to trust their mother and give her respect by honoring her wishes. When the time comes that Wilma requires more help for her own safety, her children intend to lovingly be there for her and help her get resituated.

Dealing with their aging mother has given the siblings an opportunity to get along cooperatively in their mother's best interest. They realize that forcing their mother to move would result in Wilma feeling resentful toward them. It also would undermine her self-confidence. The consequence of Wilma feeling angry and fearful would be a suppression of her immune system. Illness would soon follow, and in the end shorten her life rather than prolong it. Of course living alone increases her risk for an accident that could also result in her dying earlier. It comes down to a choice for both her and her children — love or fear. Going with the flow and allowing things to unfold as they will is a wonderful life lesson for all concerned. Choosing kindness rather than control enhances the closeness between loved ones. Whatever unknowns lie ahead, they will be dealt with appropriately at the time they happen. But for the present moment, all is well.

The most difficult lesson that aging has given Wilma is accepting her diminished ability to care for herself without assistance. She wants to maintain her independence, and resists needing help with driving, shopping, cooking, and cleaning. She also fears that she would have too much time on her hands with nothing to do. Refocusing her energies less on chores and more on having fun or social interactions with others is uncomfortable for her. Choosing enjoyable or fun activities in the present moment, rather than ruminating about the past and judging herself and others, is a challenge for Wilma.

The most difficult lesson for her children is not that they have to make difficult decisions for their mother, but rather that they are being forced to confront their own fears about aging and dying. The situation has given each child an opportunity to think about how he or she will handle these issues when they get to the point where they need help. Observing their mother's downhill course and eventual demise brings all their personal fears of death to the forefront of their minds.

*

Addiction is an issue for many people. Which form it takes, and the degree to which it intrudes into our life, varies. A genetic predisposition to having an addictive personality, combined with life's disappointments and frustrations, can result in excessive behavior. It's as if there's a void inside that needs to be filled. We may choose alcohol, food, drugs, nicotine, work, or sex to satisfy this craving.

But it doesn't really.

The psychological reason we choose excess stems from a false belief that we are not good enough. Childhood experiences of parental disapproval or abuse get distorted by our ego and turn into *self*-disapproval. "They think I'm worthless, so I must be." When life becomes difficult, we look to our substance of choice to help shore up our self-doubt … or indeed our self-loathing. Habits are formed, and addiction results.

> Tom is forty-three but looks ten years older. Life has taken its toll. A job injury thirteen years earlier began the downward spiral of pain medication and alcohol. He was bored sitting at home. Snacking and lighting up a cigarette helped pass the time. His back pain kept him from doing most activities. The sixty-pound weight gain only aggravated his condition.
>
> His life was unraveling. Laid off and feeling hopeless about ever returning to his work in construction, bills piling up, he became more irritable and withdrawn. His kids avoided him. The distance between him and his wife was growing. They hadn't been intimate for years. His gradually worsening verbal abuse, and two episodes of striking her, prompted her to threaten to take the children and leave him.
>
> Although I was the family's doctor, I seldom saw Tom. His injury and years of rehab were covered by worker's compensation. One day he appeared in my office. Unshaven, hair a mess, he sat like a lump in the chair. After he told me about his ordeal, I asked him about his feelings. His

worst fear was that he was becoming like his father. Tom remembered his father's sharp tongue and words of criticism, especially when he became drunk.

Desperately anxious that he would lose everything and everyone in his life, Tom agreed to get help. Insurance wouldn't pay for counseling, so he mustered the courage to go to his first AA meeting. He faltered several times, but he persevered. The support of the twelve-step program helped him address his anger and guilt. He learned about the importance of self-control and willpower. As he put it, "My addictions brought me to God's front door."

Abe has chosen a different path. Alcohol has always been his best friend ... and his worst nightmare. It began as fun. Everything loosened up after five beers. Handsome, now relaxed and comfortable, he found that dating and partying brought him many pleasures. He met someone, got married, and started a family. Work was okay, and he fell into his daily routines. Eventually, the responsibilities of life caught up with him—work, wife, children, and money. He tried, he really tried, to keep it all together. Gradually, over a period of twenty years, everything unraveled. Divorced, estranged from all but two of his children, and unable to hold down a permanent job, his life became empty. When he felt like no one was there for him, he could always count on a six-pack. During lucid moments of sobriety, he realized he needed to quit drinking, but despite numerous short-lived attempts, he always returned to the safety of being completely numb. One night, driving home from the bar, he slammed into a tree. Neither he nor the tree survived.

One of the most difficult addictions to conquer is to food. With tobacco, alcohol, or drugs, cutting them out of our life reduces the temptation to use them. But how does one eliminate food without perishing? Satisfying a natural instinct to feed oneself can so easily become a subconscious attempt to fill the emptiness inside by overeating or eating the wrong foods.

Eating disorders can also manifest as food avoidance. Anorexia (not eating) and bulimia (purging after eating) have become more common recently because of our society's fetish with thinness.

Crystal was a seventeen-year-old high school cheerleader who passed out twice at school. The first time it happened, she told her teachers she was having her period. The second episode prompted the school nurse to advise her mother to seek medical attention. After obtaining a thorough history and doing a physical examination, I did not find anything out of the ordinary to explain her fainting in school. I ordered some lab tests, but Crystal never got them. Six months later I received a call from the ER that Crystal had been brought in by paramedics. During cheerleading practice she had collapsed and then had a grand-mal seizure. Her laboratory tests revealed severe electrolyte abnormalities, dehydration, anemia, and malnutrition. After one night in the ICU, and another day on the medical floor, Crystal was stable enough to be discharged.

When I saw Crystal the next day in my office, she was scared and weepy. The seizure was a dramatic wake-up call that frightened her into honestly revealing what she had been doing for the last year. In her desire to be thin, Crystal had begun dieting. Mom had years of experience with diets, so the two of them began a program of reduced calories and daily workouts. Her mother was delighted to be sharing something with her teenage daughter. Unbeknownst to Mom, Crystal began taking the weight loss program to an extreme. She began skipping meals and drinking more diet cola to give her energy. No one knew, but she began purging when she felt bloated after a meal. After six months, even a small portion of food felt uncomfortable in her stomach, prompting a visit to the bathroom to relieve her perceived abdominal distention.

I attempted to explain to both her mother and Crystal how dangerous her eating disorder had become. Although they agreed that things had gotten out of hand, I sensed that they both thought I was exaggerating and that they had just gotten a little too carried away with dieting. Indeed, Crystal's response when I told her she was underweight was "Are you kidding me? I'm still too fat!" Crystal never saw the therapist I sent her to, and never came back to see me.

The underlying environmental and genetic influences that lead to addictions have a strong hold on our psyche, making it a difficult challenge for anyone coping with this issue. Crystal's reaction to the problem is fairly typical. There are times, however, when a patient is successful in overcoming his or her persistent urge to overindulge.

The first time I met Katie, I was impressed with her pleasant demeanor. Soft spoken, polite, and smiling, one could not help but like this woman. I noticed that she refused to allow my nurse to weigh her. When I asked her about it, she responded, "I don't really want to talk about it. I'm disappointed in myself — I look fat!" Katie looked healthy and fit, and I told her so. She disagreed and changed the subject.

A year later Katie's mother got very ill and almost died. Katie repeatedly blamed herself for not keeping a closer eye on her. During the months it took for her mother to recover in an extended care facility, Katie had frequent office visits for respiratory infections, fatigue and difficulty sleeping. What upset her the most, however, was her progressive weight gain.

Memories of hormone-induced teenage rounded hips, and her mother's constant disapproval, haunted her. Her mother had repeatedly cautioned her that being curvaceous would excite the boys, and that all men ever wanted from women was sex. It seemed to Katie like every gained pound made the scarlet letter across her bosom even more prominent.

Katie's mother died two years later. Approximately four months after her mom's passing, I was awakened by a call from the ER that Katie was brought in after passing out in the grocery store. I rushed to the hospital, and was shocked when I saw her gaunt body lying immobile in the hospital bed. During rounds the next morning, her guard down, she confessed her hidden secret — her obsession with her weight, her childhood expectations of being the "perfect little girl," her adolescent dieting, and her episodic purging after a "sinfully scrumptious" meal … and all the while, her constant self-loathing. That morning, as I sat on her hospital bed, Katie finally confronted her low self-esteem and her perpetual self-criticism. Between tears of shame and gasps of disapproval, her catharsis more spiritual that physical, Katie came face-to-face with the unforgiving demon she had carried around all those years.

It has taken Katie years of cognitive therapy to address the underlying psychological false beliefs that contributed to her thinking so badly about herself. She now understands how her mother's neuroses influenced her during her impressionable childhood. Katie has established a good balance between eating nutritiously and exercising almost every day. Her weight is stable, her attitude is much more positive, and her relationship with her own daughter is supportive and loving, less fraught with maternal criticism and control. Katie has successfully come to terms with the lessons of self-love and acceptance. She freely admits that negative feelings about her appearance and her worthiness as a wife and mother still come up, but less often. She has learned how to change her critical thoughts and feelings into kinder and gentler self-talk. Katie is proud of herself now, empowered by her triumph over her issues with food and her need for external approval.

Most of us overindulge in one thing or another, with its effect varying from annoyance that clothes don't fit anymore, to falling into the abyss of harmful self-destruction. Regardless, the lessons remain the same. Can I love myself enough to stop hurting myself? Can my love for others who are close to me empower me to change behaviors that are harming them? Can I see my worthiness despite what my parents said about me, and what I now believe about myself? Do I have the willpower to exert self-control? Do I have enough personal integrity to appreciate that I am a beautiful child of God—imperfect to be sure, yet from a spiritual perspective, worthy enough to successfully deal with my individual challenges? Will I be strong enough to confront my demons? Can I find the courage to risk disappointment and possible failure?

Life gives us many opportunities to learn our lessons. Each day, each situation, each interpersonal interaction, affords us a chance to deal with our issues. Yesterday's self-disappointment occurred yesterday. What about today? Will *today* be the day I finally realize that my imperfections do not make me unworthy of God's love? Spiritual love, agape, is unconditional. Those grappling with addiction need to learn to love themselves as much as God loves them. Unworthiness is human generated, not divine. Self-destructive behaviors can be modified once we accept our underlying spiritual goodness. As we begin to find a center on the worthy-unworthy continuum, we regain the personal power to stop indulging in any addictive substance to excess. Harming oneself becomes unacceptable. Our body, being the temple of our soul, takes on a sacredness that precludes self-abuse. For most of us, it takes decades to achieve this self-love, if we ever do.

*

Anger, rage, and violence consume everything they touch with fiery destruction and self-destruction. Medical science has been able to determine how genetically induced chemical imbalances of neurotransmitters in the brain predispose an individual to be more reactive in emotional situations. Environmental influences also contribute to how we interact with the world—we tend to do what was modeled for us. Abused children often become abusers of children.

The more that anger is present in our life, the more important it is for us to address this basic human emotion from both a psychological and spiritual perspective. Anger management requires an understanding of the childhood experiences that have made us so angry to begin with. Angry adults start out as angry children. Being on the receiving end of anger generates a great deal of resentment. Children will either display their feelings outwardly as unsociable acting-out behaviors or internalize them as depression, guilt, or self-loathing. The child who is emotionally, physically, or sexually abused grows up to be strong enough to then take it out on others. And so the vicious cycle of violence becomes perpetuated.

From a spiritual viewpoint, the drama of anger and violence offers aware individuals an opportunity to break this cycle and progress positively toward a better life for themselves and those around them.

> Kent is twenty-nine and in his prime. He is a nice young man with a good job and a girlfriend who loves him very much. Everything is fine as long as he is sober. Six beers turn Kent into a belligerent and violent aggressor. He has gotten into many barroom brawls, broken several bones, suffered numerous hangovers, and sabotaged four personal relationships over the years.

His second DUI was his wake-up call. Losing his driver's license would cost him his job and jeopardize future employment elsewhere. Out of desperation, motivated by the all-too-real threat of losing his livelihood and his fifth girlfriend, Kent decided to face his demon. He has been to a few AA meetings, but he doesn't like going. He has stopped drinking, however, and so far remains sober. I referred him to a marriage and family therapist, and to his credit Kent continues to see her regularly. He stopped going to bars, which by itself has had the most profound effect by removing the one activity that most frequently got him into trouble.

He promised his therapist and me that he would join a gym, and he did. Pumping iron is a good alternative to pummeling or being pummeled. Kent began to realize that his reckless behaviors and rebellious attitude were also manifestations of anger. Therapy taught him several ways of handling his angry feelings in a nonviolent manner. Talking in therapy and reading a few books gave him a better understanding of not just his anger, but how his father's unabated anger profoundly influenced the formation of Kent's rage.

The primary emotion behind anger is fear. Being afraid for your physical and emotional safety as a child results in the formation of self-protective behaviors. Anger allows individuals to protect themselves from danger. By building up enough anger, children growing up in abusive homes can pump themselves up sufficiently to overcome their fear. Long after the scary situations have passed, the learned behavior of anger remains as an ego-generated fight-or-flight defensive posture. After many years, anger becomes a reflex reaction whenever we feel afraid.

Beneath the surface, fear is always lurking, making fear our constant companion. Unconsciously our minds are continuously vigilant for anything threatening.

Love is the antidote to fear.

The spiritual lesson behind anger and violence revolves around love—love for self and love for others. It requires numerous attempts to change our angry words and actions so that we can succeed in replacing harshness with kindness. If we can stop it when we become consciously aware that we are feeling, speaking, or behaving angrily, we will break the vicious cycle of anger leading to violence. Anger management begins with a desire to not be so angry. Anger has gotten us in trouble, and we are finally motivated to change it. It will take years of practicing lovingkindness toward others, and most important, ourselves, to feel sufficiently in control of this powerful emotion.

Eventually we will reach a level of understanding that permist us to work on the lesson of forgiveness. Realizing that we are *all* flawed, that we *all* have many lessons to learn in this lifetime, allows us to not be so hard on ourselves and others. By intending to be kinder, and succeeding at doing so more and more often, we can begin to let go of self-judgment. We can forgive our inner child for doing what comes naturally—self-protection.

Once we are able to begin to forgive ourselves, the next step is to work on forgiving those who have harmed us with their anger and abuse. Realizing that others have hurt us because they were hurt by others gives us a greater understanding of the larger cosmic and karmic picture. The *only* way out of this repetitive pattern is love. It is through love that we find a way to reduce the oppressive effects of anger.

*

We come into adulthood with a load of baggage. Childhood circumstances cause the emotional wounds that strongly influence the formation of issues we will need to address as adults. For some children the psychological trauma is overwhelming, resulting in an emotional retreat inward. Although they may function adequately in the real world, something inside has withered.

> Joan is a fifty-year-old married woman with two children in college. Basically a healthy woman, I see her infrequently. She doesn't like to complain much and tends to minimize her symptoms. When I inquire about her health, she usually says, "Well you know doctor, I'm a bit nervous and have trouble sleeping at night, but I manage just fine." She doesn't ask for medication for these problems.

> Joan is a petite woman who makes herself smaller with her rounded shoulders and her soft-spoken demeanor. Meek, apologetic, frequently gazing downward, she further manages to not draw attention to herself by never wearing makeup or styling her graying brown hair. She prefers to avoid other people, venturing out only to go to work or run errands. Joan's parents divorced when she was six years old. She once confided in me that her stepfather fondled her inappropriately, but she had no memory of incest. She married a domineering, nonaffectionate, egotistical man who is incapable of nurturing her. Indeed, he often ridicules her in front of others, and she takes it.

> There is a sadness and resignation about Joan that has prompted me on several occasions to initiate a discussion about the apparent absence of happiness and joy in her life. When I shared my concerns about her self-esteem and the need for her to love and value herself, she smiled politely and said, "I know, but I'm not ready to deal with all that right now."

Joan is burdened by her life's experiences. Abandoned by her daddy, abused by her stepfather, she entered adult life feeling unworthy and unlovable. She felt powerless and inferior, an easy mark for the fast-talking man she eventually married. In subtle and nonsubtle ways he has been able to humiliate and oppress her. Joan has become a dependent woman, a helpless martyr, who manages to get through every day, but does so devoid of hope or life-affirming energy. Despite being offered alternatives to her current situation, Joan has repeatedly refused psychological counseling. She would rather be passive and accept her life as it is than rock the boat and incur her husband's anger and rejection.

*

I can personally attest to the benefits, and challenges, of having a Type A personality. It got me into, and through, medical school. The determined striving for perfection and the ability to efficiently multitask contributed to my success. But the impatient, controlling, driven, and angry aspect of Type A-ness has detracted from my happiness and caused problems in my interpersonal relationships. I have worked and continue to work, on this side of my personality. Recognizing Type A behaviors in myself allows me to readily see it in others.

> Jason is a forty-two-year-old stockbroker. I don't see him often—he doesn't have time in his busy schedule. When not at work he is usually on the phone. He bought one of those handless earphones and was truly in seventh heaven. If he has to wait more than fifteen minutes for me, he starts walking around the office asking the staff how much longer it will be. Which is funny, because he is invariably ten minutes or more late for his appointments. Jason often uses a doctor's visit as a chance to also do four or five other tasks from his never-ending list of things to do. Hence the tardiness for his appointments with me.

> I see Jason twice a year to monitor his hypertension and cholesterol. He insists on lab tests every six months, and an

office visit exactly three days later. Whenever his results are even a little above the normal range, he gets very angry. He demands perfection of himself, and all those around him. Despite being financially successful, married to a lovely woman, having two children who adore him, and living in an upscale home with lots of "toys", Jason is still not satisfied. It's as if he still hasn't found what he's looking for, and is still searching for some ideal perfection.

Frustration, disappointment, or having to wait, all resulted in the same emotion—anger. In order to demonstrate the harmful effects his anger was having on his heart, I put a blood pressure cuff on his arm and left it in place while I started a conversation with him about a topic that I knew would make him very upset. Every five minutes I took his blood pressure and pulse. When he saw how quickly they both escalated, he was amazed. He had a sudden flash of insight. Now he understood my concerns about his increased risk of a heart attack or a stroke. He looked straight into my eyes and said, "Okay, doc, let's deal with this now!"

After I had spent years trying to persuade him to be more physically active, he finally took it to heart. He began a daily regimen of a few stretches, and then got on the treadmill for thirty minutes (while watching the news, of course). I taught him a simple breathing exercise that he would do while driving, waiting in line (or in my office), and as he was falling asleep. Occasionally he actually started slow deep breathing when he noticed himself getting angry. He is making a conscious effort to slow down, to be more patient, and to be less controlling. He has begun to prioritize his list of to-do's, learning to be more calm while doing them. He is now aware of staying on task and on time.

The combination of daily aerobic exercise, slow deep breathing, and modifying his reactive angry behavior, has resulted in Jason getting off his hypertension medication. He has lost fifteen pounds, and his cholesterol levels have dropped. Most important, Jason is happier. He is finding that balance between work and family, being productive and being playful. These days, it is actually a pleasure to see him in my office.

*

Our society values money and success. In our pursuit of these, most of us live a fast-paced life, juggling many responsibilities simultaneously. This constant stress results in a barrage of adrenalin and other stress hormones that take their toll on our body and our mind. We get so caught up with our daily routines that we seldom take a breather to *not do*. It usually requires our body to break down, burdened by self-imposed *shoulds,* to force us to confront the consequences of our stressful lives.

> George is a very busy man. No sooner do his eyes open than he is mentally reviewing the list of things he needs to do that day. In the process of prioritizing his schedule, he notices those familiar cramping sensations in his lower abdomen that signal the first of three bowel movements he has every morning. What he fails to notice is the rhythmic clenching of his jaws. Not until the muscle tension builds up enough to develop into a dull headache does he take notice. This usually prompts him to take his customary two ibuprofen with his first cup of coffee.
>
> It is impressive to observe the efficiency with which George goes through his morning routine: putting the dog out with his bowl of food; organizing his briefcase as he boots up his laptop to check his e-mail; standing in the kitchen eating breakfast while taking his handful of vitamin supplements;

taking his three-minute shower once he had his third bowel movement; dressing in the clothes he picked out the night before; and going out the front door as his children are just getting up for school.

His work requires many phone calls interspersed with numerous meetings, driving around town to meet customers and run errands, making several pit stops for lunch and his four large colas. He usually gets home too late to have supper with the family, choosing instead to heat up his dinner in the microwave and eat quickly while watching TV or checking his laptop.

Weekends fly by, filled with home repairs, watching the kids' soccer games or dance recitals, and going to the gym for two hours for his weekly workout. People are often more available on the weekend, so he spends several hours conducting transactions from home. George loves his cell phone. It allows him to stay connected with his business world even when he's away from the office. The family just takes it for granted when Dad walks off with phone to ear while they have fun.

George didn't notice that his children and wife were slowly drifting away, emotionally detaching from him as he had systematically withdrawn from them. What he did notice was the nagging chest pains that hit him periodically. At first the chewable antacids gave him relief. But it took a two-hour episode of unremitting discomfort and shortness of breath to prompt a midnight trip to the ER, and subsequent admission to the hospital, to rule out a heart attack.

The work-up revealed many stress-induced ailments typical of driven individuals. His chest pains turned out to be both cardiac and gastric. Anxiety was precipitating both spasm of his coronary arteries (angina) and stomach acid reflux. His blood pressure was elevated, his heart had irregular skipped beats, and there were early signs of coronary artery blockages. The nurses noted his twitching legs and fitful sleep. A sleep study was ordered revealing restless leg syndrome, sleep apnea, a dangerously slow heart rate, and diminished oxygen saturation. No wonder he was exhausted all the time—his mind never allowed his body to rest. George was shocked at the extent of the damage his body had endured. After I explained the mind-body connection and the mechanism by which stress had caused his medical problems, he began to understand what he was doing to himself.

For several weeks after his hospitalization George made an effort to slow down and get home earlier. Because he was used to constant activity, physical or mental, slow equaled boring. It took about a month before George returned to his hectic pattern of existence. Rather than gradually modify his Type A behavior to find the balance between activity and hyperactivity, he chose to return to familiar ways. Medication had reduced the severity of his physical symptoms so he was less distracted by discomfort. Initially the family spent more time together, but that didn't last long. His relationships with his significant others had become familiar and comfortable—at least more comfortable than all the necessary changes that would be required to rejuvenate the intimacy they had once had.

It has been three years since George was hospitalized. Because he had fewer symptoms, I began to see him less often. Forgetting to take his prescriptions resulted in pain, so he became fairly diligent about taking them. The family remains intact, everyone continuing to live out their lives as before. Illness and pain brought George the gift of insight. It became apparent that stress and his Type A personality were causing him physical and emotional discomfort. Despite this awareness, from outward appearances, it may seem that nothing of significance has changed.

It takes looking into George's eyes to notice the subtle shift that has occurred. The spark is gone. His frenzied life may have caused medical problems, but it also gave him a zest that was energizing and pleasurable. The hustle and bustle was his life, and he couldn't give it up. Without it he was bored. He now knows that stress will shorten his life...he just doesn't care anymore. At a subconscious level, this knowledge has drained him of his inner drive. He is depressed that things have turned out the way they have. He sees himself as a failure. He feels lonely, still, but now not even work satisfies his need for excitement. The knowledge that stress will negatively affect the quality and duration of his life has not resulted in an epiphany of change or inner growth, but instead fear and dread about his future. He continues to go through the motions of his life, but something is gone. Opportunity presented itself, but George chose the easier course. Growth is always more difficult. If we wait too long to face the reality of our life and make the necessary adjustments to bring inner fulfillment, the task seems overwhelming and impossible to achieve. We give up. We die inside. We simply go on out of habit. Eventually death becomes a blessing, a way out of the quiet desperation.

*

The effects of depression on the physical body are widespread. The chemical imbalance in the brain that results in depression affects the entire body because receptor sites for brain neurochemicals exist in every organ. The consequences of years of depression is a gradual reduction in the ability of each organ to perform its specific function, making emotional "dis-ease" a prime cause for physical illness. The immune system is especially sensitive to the brain neurotransmitters. A suppressed immunity can result in a new cancerous growth going undetected. Chronic depression, therefore, will increase the likelihood for the formation of cancer in those individuals genetically predisposed to cancer.

Sol was a self-made man. He was an immigrant from Eastern Europe, took evening classes while working in the daytime, graduated law school, and got married and raised a family. By every standard Sol was living the American dream. Through hard work and determined persistence he moved out of the ghetto into middle-class success.

Despite outward appearances, Sol was not happy. He loved his wife and sons, and he appreciated his good life. Yet every day brought hours of anguish and dread. He would wake up every night after four or five hours of sleep and go into his study. While chain smoking, he would spend hours ruminating about his concerns. Fear was foremost in his mind. He worried about everything: his health, the safety of his wife and children, strangers walking toward him on the street, losing his money in the stock market, death. Although medication would have alleviated his anxiety and the incessant doom-and-gloom scenarios he replayed in his head, he did not trust doctors or their medicines.

Depression set in after he turned fifty. He thought of himself as a failure. Rather than appreciate all that he had and all that he had accomplished in his life, Sol withdrew into his world of inner turmoil. He felt isolated and afraid. His symptoms intensified with age, but he shunned all suggestions by the family to seek help.

One morning a terrifying episode of acute shortness of breath and swelling of his face and neck forced him to consent to go to the hospital. Lung cancer had insidiously grown around the blood vessels in his upper chest precipitating a medical emergency. Within twenty-four hours the diagnosis was established and treatment was initiated. Sol's worst fear, cancer, had materialized. He reluctantly tried radiation and chemotherapy, but stopped treatments once the acute swelling and shortness of breath subsided. The side effects were intolerable to him. All he wanted to do was die, but thoughts of death petrified him. When I came by Sol's hospital room before discharge, he grabbed my arm and drew me close to him. "Can't you give me something in the IV to kill me fast so I don't have to suffer?" The terror in his eyes, the pleading in his voice, the strength of his grip. For a moment we looked deeply into each others eyes. This was not the first time someone had asked me to assist them to die quickly. "I'm sorry Dad, I can't do that."

Sol died six weeks later. The oppressive anxiety and depression that had ravaged his life plagued him till his death. He died as he lived ... in fear.

Like all of us, Sol's life was a mixture of accomplishments and disappointments. His anxiety neutralized any joy he may have felt from his successes, and intensified the self-judgment of his perceived failures. Fear drained his vital energy, leaving an emptiness that left him hollow inside.

If Sol had made one simple choice in his life, to be willing to love himself, his genetic predisposition to anxiety and depression could not have consumed him. If when facing his apprehensions about failure, pain, and death, Sol had felt supported and protected, he would have been able to overcome his self-doubt. But his parents died when he was young, and he did not feel safe. Religion provided him no comfort. His intellect prevented him from believing anything that was intangible. And so he suffered.

Many lessons were offered to both father and son during Sol's end of life. Sol was given an opportunity to finally come to terms with fear, but it was too late. A life-long pattern of anxiety and depression was not going to magically change. In fact, dying only intensified his emotions. There was no deathbed epiphany—just fear.

For his son, there were many lessons as well. Watching someone you love die, and being powerless to alter the course of events, is a humbling experience. Allowing rather than controlling. There was a desire for me to talk about all those things that were still unresolved, issues between a child and his parent. But somehow most of them never really got settled. As a physician who deals with death and dying every working day, I found that experiencing it on a personal level was profound. I was surprised by the intensity of my feelings. I expected that because intellectually and spiritually I was okay with his passing, emotions such as sadness and anger would not hit me as hard. Boy, was I wrong! And then there's the lesson of how does a son say no to a father's request.

We all experience fear. Earthschool is often a scary place. Courage is necessary to get past our fears so that we may take the risk to challenge ourselves to grow. Those children who grow up in a more nurturing environment are better able to find the strength from within to address the difficult issues in their lives. For those who did not receive adequate parental love and guidance, understanding and accepting the concept that another source of encouragement is available to them, from their Higher self and their Higher Power, allowing them to transcend their fears, eludes them. Once we realize how deeply we are loved by Invisible Energy, we will have the personal power to achieve *anything*.

Although we may feel inadequate to attain our desired goals, accepting love from our soul, and the soul of God, will provide the impetus to reach for the golden ring … all the while willing to accept whatever the outcome is without self-flagellation. Love becomes the alternative to fear. Love is the shield that protects against the depression that results from self-criticism. All we need is love. Love is all we need.

*   *   *

As human beings evolve spiritually, milestones of growth become evident. *Young souls* are dealing predominantly with issues of survival. They are fearful there may not be enough for sustenance, seeing others as rivals vying for what resources are available. They tend to focus concretely on the physical plane of existence. They view psychological and spiritual issues as superfluous and irrelevant to their primary task of getting through each day intact. Harming others to achieve success is a necessary evil, a means to an end. They are quick to blame, often using shame, fear, and humiliation to manipulate others. Feeling competitive, dissatisfied, and alienated most of the time, they take pleasure in beating someone else.

Spiritual evolution requires lifetimes of struggling with the basics of subsistence advantageously, permitting sufficient safety from danger to allow expansion into higher realms of human consciousness. Coping every day with survival distracts a person from putting energy into personal or spiritual growth. Lower vibrational energies such as fear, anger, desire, and selfishness progress gradually, over many lifetimes, to love, empathy, and generosity. As we evolve, cooperation and peaceful coexistence achieve greater importance. There is an appreciation of commonality among all sentient beings. Love becomes the dominant emotion, with thoughts for others being as important and satisfying as personal gratification. For *old souls,* spiritual advancement surpasses pain avoidance as a higher priority, discomfort and illness taking on the added dimension of opportunity for growth. Difficulties become lessons, suffering dissipates.

We begin to see patterns or themes to our lives that transcend ordinary daily occurrences. A big picture emerges encompassing self, others, and the ethereal. Appreciation for lessons to be learned gives meaning to our lives and understanding to personal difficulties. Life becomes less scary and more challenging. Possibilities, with time, become actualities.

Awareness is the key to beginning the journey toward wholeness. Noticing negative feelings, thoughts, or behaviors within us brings our attention to the dozen or so dominant challenges we have chosen to deal with in this lifetime. Observing emotions such as anger, hatred, jealousy, anxiety, or depression alerts us to underlying matters to be explored. Thoughts concerning low self-esteem and controlling or harming others illuminate areas of necessary growth. Behaviors also serve as beacons highlighting areas that need scrutiny—impatience, shyness, laziness, violence, and so on. These negative emotions, thoughts, and behaviors recur frequently every day. Many situations, interactions with others, or incessant thoughts remind us of the personal issues dominant in our life. We usually deal with several items simultaneously. At any moment in time one issue is in the foreground, demanding our immediate involvement, but we observe ourselves juggling our personal set of concerns intermittently throughout each day.

Crucial to any personal or spiritual growth is the understanding that we are all imperfect beings. We need to accept our flaws as opportunities for expansion rather than reason for self-recrimination. We are all beautiful children of God. If God can love us unconditionally, despite our human imperfection, so can we. Observations of issues or problems in our life is not justification for self-judgement, but rather are to be used as a springboard to improve the quality of our life.

The challenge as we observe traits in ourselves that we prefer not to have is to bypass judging ourselves as good or bad and simply decide to change it. If at first we realize the need to change but are not prepared to address the issue presently, then at least we need to accept it as is for now without berating ourselves. Eventually we will realize that hurtful behaviors and thoughts are not consistent with our self-image as the loving human being we desire to be, motivating us to pursue the self-healing changes required for spiritual growth.

*   *   *

> *Life isn't about waiting for the storms to pass,*
> *It's about learning to dance in the rain*

*   *   *

The goal of evolving in consciousness is to experience more of the higher vibrational energies:

happiness	joy		serenity
love	harmony	nonviolence	kindness
inspiration	hopefulness		clarity
enlightenment		wisdom	
benevolence	empathy	generosity	mercy
forgiveness		nonjudgmentalness	
courage	fortitude		perseverance
temperance		self-control	
patience	acceptance		noncontrolling
responsibility		trustworthiness	
equanimity	detachment	balance	flexibility
vulnerability		humility	
assertiveness	empowerment		self-nurturing
spontaneity		zeal	
appreciation	gratefulness		thankfulness
faith		trust	

Dealing favorably with the cluster of lessons that our lives offer us gives us the opportunities to achieve more of these positive energies. Experiencing higher vibrational energies elevates our soul to a higher plane of existence, which ultimately fulfills the primary purpose for each of our lives.

*   *   *

At first glance the following list of issues and lessons may appear simplistic. However, situations in our life that seem complicated and perhaps overwhelming can easily be broken down to a few basic lessons. As we become aware of the many opportunities that arise each day to change old patterns of thoughts and behaviors, we will want to refer periodically to this list to remind us where we need to focus our attention.

ISSUE	LESSONS
Abandonment	self-love self-esteem take care of yourself know you're never alone
Abused	self-love stand up for yourself avoid abusiveness to others avoid co-dependency
Abusive	release anger lovingkindness respectfulness
Addiction	self-love release unworthiness address guilt willpower, self-control
Agitation	equanimity
Aggression	release anger release fear forgiveness love
Aging	acceptance of change endure deterioration of body and mind detachment from the physical understanding transition

ISSUE	LESSONS
Alienation	empathy
	involvement
	generosity
	hope
Anger	love
	release fear
	release resentment
	release control
Anxiety	courage
	faith
	trust
	release fear
	go with the flow
Apathy	active participation
	express emotions
Approval seeking	love yourself
	self-esteem
Argumentative	release control
	kindness
Arrogance	humility
Betrayal	protect yourself
	be more careful
	avoid self-blame
	forgiveness

ISSUE	LESSONS
Bitterness	release anger let go forgiveness
Blaming	release judgment of self & others self-love
Boredom	be in the present embrace life enthusiastically take charge of your life release fear of change
Burdened	choose to see the positive endure faith lighten-up
Callous	empathy sensitivity
Closed mindedness	expansiveness trust willingness to grow release fear of change
Competitiveness	release inadequacy love yourself as you are relax and have fun
Confusion	clarity prioritize organize focus

ISSUE	LESSONS
Congenital abnormalities	acceptance faith serenity patience flexibility unconditional love
Controlling	release fear release anger release resentment
Craving	detachment discipline moderation
Critical	love allow compassion mercy
Cruelty	release anger release fear lovingkindness
Death	let go faith release fear acceptance
Defeatism	self-love optimism hope

ISSUE	LESSONS
Demanding	humility
	respect
	release control
	release anger
Denial	acceptance
	release fear
	release control
Dependency	courage
	independence
	release fear
Depression (grieving for loss)	full expression of feelings
	acceptance of change
	faith
	release attachment
Depression (self-critical)	self-love
	self-forgiveness
	self-nurturing
Desire	detachment from the material world
	acceptance of what you have
	avoid expectations
Despair	hope
	faith
Disappointment	avoid expectations
	detachment

ISSUE	LESSONS
Discouragement	avoid expectations persistence patience
Dissatisfied	avoid expectations acceptance (of self and life)
Dominant	humility allowing release control release anger
Dread	courage avoid expectations stay in present moment
Egotistical	giving love empathy
Enabling	release control avoid co-dependency allow
Escapism	acceptance stay in present moment
Excessive	moderation
Exhaustion	self-nurturing self-love slow down

Jeffrey D. Millman, M.D.

ISSUE	LESSONS
Failure	persistence patience self-love
Fear	love
Flighty	focus/concentration patience
Frustration	patience release control acceptance
Gluttony	temperance
Gossiping	release judgment love empathy
Greed	generosity feel abundant non-materialism
Grieving	let go faith acceptance
Guilt	express feelings (especially anger) stand up for yourself loving yourself is okay

ISSUE	LESSONS
Hatred (projected self-loathing)	kindness empathy release judgment forgiveness (self and others) release anger
Helpless	assertiveness self-love courage
Hopeless	faith
Humiliation	self-love self-confidence detachment from criticism lighten-up
Hyperactive	learn stillness self-esteem avoid stimulants/sugar transmute energy (exercise)
Hypervigilant	calmness trust
Hypocrisy	truthfulness
Impatience	patience release control slow down
Inadequacy	self-love self-esteem

ISSUE	LESSONS
Incurable	acceptance positive thinking faith
Indecisive	trust and faith in self courage to take risks self-esteem release self-judgment take charge of your life
Indifferent	actively engage life be in present moment
Inferiority	self-acceptance self-love
Inflammatory	release anger
Inflexibility	release control
Insecurity	trust faith self-love
Insensitive	compassion empathy
Irritable	release anger release control
Isolation	partake of life get out of yourself release fear

ISSUE	LESSONS
Jealousy	contentment
	acceptance
	detachment
	feel abundant
	appreciation
Joyless	allow full expression of feelings
	hope
	self-worth
Judgement (self)	self-nurturing
	self-love
	lighten-up
Judgement (others)	love
	allow
	compassion
	mercy
Lack	feel abundant
	appreciation
Lazy	self-motivation
	persistence
	zeal
Lonely	you're never alone
	self-love
	release fear
	reach out

ISSUE	LESSONS
Low self-esteem	self-love forgiveness of childhood abusers courage
Lust	balance of sexuality self-control
Lying	honesty detachment from criticism release need for approval
Malnourishment	self-nurture
Martyr	self-love
Materialism	feel abundant detachment
Meek	assertiveness
Miserable	endure lighten-up appreciation
Mood swings	balance equanimity
Negativity	appreciation optimism hope

ISSUE	LESSONS
Non-trusting	trust
	faith
	release control
Oppressed	assertiveness
	courage
	self-love
Overprotective	control
	release fear
	trust
	faith
Oversensitive	release self-judgment
	self-love
Overwhelmed	choose to see the positive
	endure
	faith
	lighten-up
	do less
Pain	endure
	acceptance
	transcendence
Paranoia	release fear
	love
	trust
Passive	assertiveness
	self-love

ISSUE	LESSONS
Persecution	stand up for yourself self-worth courage
Pity	release judgment humility
Poverty	appreciation of what you *do* have detachment make better choices determination
Powerless	self-worth self-love courage
Prejudice	release judgment release fear love
Pride	humility
Procrastination	time management respect for others release fear
Punitive	release anger release judgment
Rage	release anger release fear love non-violence

ISSUE	LESSONS
Rebellious	release anger forgiveness self-love do no harm (kindness) take charge of *your* life
Reckless	self-love value life moderation resist selfishness
Regret	forgiveness let go stay in present moment
Rejection	self-love faith you're not alone
Remorse	forgiveness let go release guilt
Repressed	express feelings freely self-worth control
Resentment	let go forgiveness
Resistance	allow faith

ISSUE	LESSONS
Sadistic	love (self and others) release anger forgiveness (of abusers)
Sadness	hope acceptance of change faith lighten-up
Secretive	trust
Self-destructive	self-love forgiveness (self and others) acceptance
Self-hatred	self-love
Self-pity	take responsibility release judgment get out of yourself
Self-punishment	self-love
Sexual disinterest	self-love forgiveness (of abusers) self-worth okay to have fun
Sexual inadequacy	release attachment to physical release need for approval self-acceptance

ISSUE	LESSONS
Shame	self-love
	let go
	accepting responsibility
	release judgment
Spiteful	release resentment
	lovingkindness
Stinginess	feel abundant
Stress	(see anxiety, fear, Type A)
Struggling	allow
	let go
Stubborn	flexibility
Suffering	endure
	release resistance
Suicidal	value life
	self-love
	hope
	endure
Tense	relax
	be in and enjoy present moment
	release fear
Terrified	trust
	courage
	love

ISSUE	LESSONS
Trapped	assertiveness
	take responsibility (for self)
	self-love
Type A	balance
	calmness
	patience
	control
	prioritizing
	accepting of self-imperfection
Unappreciated	self-love
	self-approval
	self-esteem
Unappreciative	gratefulness
Unbalanced	moderation
	equanimity
Uncreative	get beyond rational mind
	release rigidity
	be lighthearted
Unforgiving	forgiveness
	let go
	take risks
Unfulfilled	take charge of your life
	take risks
	release fear
	self-love

ISSUE	LESSONS
Used	stand up for yourself
Vagueness	focus
Vanity	humility attachment to the material *genuine* self-love
Vengeful	lovingkindness release anger release fear release judgment
Victimization	resist blaming others for *your* choices take responsibility assertiveness
Vindictive	love release anger
Violence	love (self and others) release anger release fear forgiveness
Vulnerable	self-empowerment courage trust faith
Wasteful	moderation appreciation

Jeffrey D. Millman, M.D.

ISSUE	LESSONS
Weak	assertiveness
Weight (over)	self-love moderation be more active
Weight (under)	self-nurturing self-acceptance stillness
Withdrawal	partake of life get out of yourself release fear take risks
Worry	courage faith trust stay in present moment

Chapter 6

Transition

All living things die.

Immutable.

When we die, our physical body ceases to function as a living organism. Our corporeal existence on this three-dimensional plane ends. Left to its own devices, the body would putrefy and decay. Human society has chosen to bury or burn the physical remains.

Whereas death implies an ending of a life, the word *transition* describes more accurately what occurs when we die, which is a passage of consciousness from one reality to another. *Transition* is the appropriate term for soul movement in and out of a body. It is a portal to the other side, and back again. Back and forth. Ebb and flow.

Birth and death share much in common. Birth requires passage through a narrow tunnel toward bright light. Innumerable accounts of dying report passage through a narrow tunnel toward a bright Light. When born, we meet with other humans. Upon death, we meet with other human souls who died before us. Pain accompanies both aspects of transition. Birth is painful to both mother and child.

Mother's pain is obvious, but imagine the extreme pressure on the baby's head and body passing through the birth canal. Similarly, dying is painful. Whether we linger through the process or by God's grace go quickly, pain is present. Once the soul is released from the confines of its material body, all pain stops immediately. The blind can see, the deaf can hear, and all the physical encumbrances and limitations experienced in life no longer exist. Pain is perceived only by the brain and the five senses. Once free of the body, the spirit becomes free of pain.

When interviewed, many who have touched the other side and returned relay specific details of events and sensations they experienced while they were clinically dead. Raymond Moody, MD, did pioneer research on near-death and death experiences by interviewing approximately three thousand people who were pronounced dead and were subsequently revived. I have combined the details reported to him, and described in his book *Life After Life*, with the personal accounts related to me from more than a dozen of my patients, to summarize what takes place as a person makes the transition from this reality to the next.

> As the pain becomes intensely unbearable, a loud buzzing noise occurs accompanied by rapid passage through a long, dark tunnel. Suddenly they are hovering over their body, painlessly observing someone aggressively administering CPR or witnessing themselves unconscious or bleeding profusely.

> Emotionally they often feel upset or confused. Other souls important in their lives who had died previously come to comfort and reassure them. An intense but not blinding bright light appears, often described as a benevolent being, asking telepathically a question that sets in motion a life review. Visual images appear rapidly and vividly, accompanied by the emotions of the event,

presented nonjudgmentally with the intent to educate. This highlighting of the prominent circumstances in their lives prompts reflection about two prominent issues relevant to the human experience — learning about love and acquiring knowledge. Despite an urge to proceed further, the individuals are advised to stop, and to return to their body. They are told it is not their time to die, that they still have things to accomplish and people who still need them. Immersed in the peaceful and loving environment of the afterlife, they are reluctant to go back into their body, relishing the beauty and serenity of the experience. Suddenly they find themselves reunited with their physical body and once again in pain.

These death experiences appear to be only the first level that souls encounter after release from physical form. *The Tibetan Book of the Dead* describes eight *bardos,* or stages, that souls follow after dying. Strikingly, the first bardo is very similar to the near-death experience described above. The last or eighth bardo is reincarnation into the next life, thereby bringing the process full circle.

The details of the afterlife are less important than the overall concept. Death is not an end. It is only the beginning of another process that has been labeled "death" but that is in reality a different form of "life". Energy cannot be created or destroyed, merely transmuted. Form will change, the body will decompose, but the life force energy within it has an existence unto itself, capable of entrance and exit from one state of being into another, from life to afterlife.

There are a multitude of reports of less intense out-of-body experiences that begin similarly but usually do not proceed as far along. The person hovers painlessly, capable of hearing and seeing all that occurs, but rejoins the body before progressing toward the Light. Extreme pain is what usually precipitates this experience of leaving the body temporarily.

The skeptical and cynical explain these experiences as hallucinations brought on by oxygen deprivation. So why is everyone having basically the same hallucination? Besides, many such occurrences happen very quickly after the heart and the lungs stop functioning and therefore before oxygen saturation in the brain diminishes. Scientifically these accounts are considered anecdotal and lack reproducible double-blind analysis. Current medical technology lacks the sophistication to detect and measure soul transition. And how would you perform a double-blind study on death anyway?

Once again we are faced with a free will decision to either make the leap of faith or not. For those of you with an emerging sixth sense that facilitates connection with your inner wisdom, it becomes less an act of faith and more an intuitive knowing … unprovable scientifically yet part of *your truth*.

The events described in these experiences reflect the passage of the life force going out and then coming back into a physical body. Soul-body fusion loosens but never quite detaches. The invisible connection is capable of "stretching", freeing our soul energy to explore realms other than three-dimensional reality. Time and space become irrelevant. Out-of-body occurrences, near-death and other altered states of reality experienced through meditation, prayer, hypnosis, dreaming, and hallucinogens, all result in disassociation of soul from body to varying degrees, but *not completely*. If it did, death would ensue.

As a physician I have personally witnessed the movement of life force energy, or chi, from the celestial plane into a physical form, and from the body back to whence souls abide between lives. Early one morning, having just delivered a stillborn infant boy, holding it in my arms doing CPR while the nurse suctioned the mucus and administered oxygen, there was a sudden jolt. The baby flung its arms and legs out, took in a large breath of air, and began screaming like a banshee. I felt the soul enter its body. Likewise, I have been present when spirit left. As a medical student, while on call, I was summoned to the bedside of a comatose older woman. Death was expected and imminent. I sat there several minutes, holding her motionless hand. She took two or three more gasps of air. With her last breath I strongly sensed something pass out of her body toward the ceiling. Honestly, it freaked me out a bit. Out-of-body, near-death, and death experiences were not discussed or taught to medical students in 1970. It was an awakening in my scientific mind to the presence of Invisible Energy.

As the soul sheds itself of its deceased body, it simultaneously releases the ego. Ego is acquired and developed as protection from the pains of life. Generated by the self, the ego no longer is necessary once self dies. Higher self, that individual spark of Light that inhabits a physical body temporarily, returns to the peaceful wonderment of the other side ego free. Fear-generated neuroses dissipate once exposed to the love of the Light. That which we label *personality,* the thoughts and emotions that individuate each of us uniquely, appears to persist during the early transition phase. How much of the personality is completely shed, and what traits persist into the next incarnation, is not clear. Some philosophies envision our soul as a drop of water returning to the sea, losing its identity completely in the process. Past-life regression implies a continuity of personality that forms the template of life lessons still unlearned that carries over into the next life.

* * *

Coma presents an interesting phenomenon. Although the basic functions of living are being carried out, the conscious mind is not engaged. Respiration, circulation, digestion, and so on continue on their own, or with external technological assistance, but cognitive functions are absent. Brain wave EEG activity persists, albeit in an altered pattern, indicating that basic neurological functioning remains intact. However, we can talk to, shake, or even pinch a comatose person without an observable response.

Like out-of-body experiences, coma is a separation of spirit from physical, distinguished from death in that a minimal connection persists preventing permanent severance. Although the soul detaches sufficiently to experience the reality of the other side, a lifeline remains, supplying enough life force to sustain vital functions.

There is a physical and spiritual component to the comatose state. Physically, loss of consciousness may be initiated by swelling and damage to the brain due to injury or a stroke, by a temporary lack of blood flow during shock or bleeding, or as an escape from the pain of trauma. Simultaneously, the individual is having a near-death experience. The soul has an opportunity to embark upon a life review and assessment. Afterward, the decision to return and merge again fully with the physical body can require complex evaluation and assistance from Invisible Energy. This process can last from hours to days or even weeks. A period of time is also necessary for physical repair of injured or damaged organs. Coma is a benign way the universe has of permitting detachment from the pain of recuperation.

People can lapse in and out of coma. It is as if they are straddling the fence of life, with one "leg" on either side. While conscious, they experience pain and can interact with us, even if only at a primal reflexive level. While unconscious, they are experiencing the other side, free of pain, and with a clarity that is impossible with all the distractions of the mundane world. As individuals drift from coma to a more awake state, they often act as if they see other entities in the room, possessing momentarily a clairvoyant ability to sense souls now deceased who were important in their life. These disembodied spirits are drawn to the comatose person to assist in the process.

Modern science can allow the soul and body to buy enough time to choose life or death. Some on life support recover in a short period of time, with varying degrees of residual disability and medical complications ranging from mild to serious. Others languish in a coma longer, with biological functions dwindling and more heroic technological support being required. Healthcare providers and family members eventually have to decide whether to maintain a persistent vegetative condition at all costs, or wean the person off the machines. When life support is gradually removed, most pass painlessly away, although some miraculously manage to survive. Coma allows all involved, patient and loved ones, time to adjust to the transition of the individual to the other side.

Although there is no perception of pain while unconscious, there is awareness of events and other people. While hovering, the comatose are capable of hearing and seeing everything around them. Therefore, it is recommended that we talk to the person in a coma as if they are fully present. Give words of encouragement, pray with them, and tell them how much you love them. Sometimes patients are asked to come back and join the living once again, but it is the ultimate in selfless love to accept the wisdom of Divine will and to end all requests with, "Do what is best for your spiritual growth."

As a person lapses in and out of a comatose state, a wonderful opportunity is being presented to enhance spiritual growth. Great insight can be achieved around the time of transition. As one is dying, the veils of illusion part, allowing a *higher wisdom* to prevail. Awarenesses achieved at or around death are as valid to spiritual advancement as any insight learned during previous difficulties in life. It is less relevant when or how growth is achieved than that it is achieved. A dying person may blurt out a seemingly random statement or call out the name of a deceased loved one. If you pay attention to what is being said, give it credibility, and don't just attribute it to the babbling of a dying person, you become a facilitator for soul growth.

Simply encourage him or her by asking appropriate questions, such as to describe who or what they are "seeing". Sometimes reflective listening, where you mirror back what the person says by rewording it, is helpful. By so doing you can expedite this special opportunity for spiritual expansion.

> Agnes was experiencing a near-death encounter with her deceased husband as she lay on her deathbed. I happened to be making my final house call that evening. She opened her eyes wider as she started to mumble something about Archie.
>
> "Do you see Archie?" I said.
>
> "He's so handsome," she responded.
>
> "What is he saying?" I asked.
>
> "Come to me," she said. "I so much want to be with him, but I'm afraid."
>
> I then said, "It sounds like you're ready to join him. It's okay to go, Agnes. We love you. We'll be fine. You don't have to be afraid. Archie is with you."
>
> Her two children and their spouses stayed with her in her bedroom after I left. I spoke to Agnes's daughter the next morning. For about twenty minutes Agnes and her loved ones spoke occasionally as she continued to interact with Archie. She then drifted off. As her body was shutting down, the four of them continued to sit with her, sharing with one another the experience of the moment. None of them had ever witnessed the dying process before. Agnes's transition became a truly spiritual experience for all of them. She died peacefully that night.

Grieving families waiting for the outcome of their loved one's comatose state can take comfort and have faith that everything is happening for a purpose and that Cosmic Energy is very present during times of transition, assisting at an invisible level. The experience of having a loved one in a coma is a multifaceted opportunity to learn about love … the love of doing everything possible to facilitate healing in another being, and the love to let go if passing over is inevitable. As we deal with the possibility that our loved one may die, we must come to terms with all that transition involves—loss, abandonment, unfinished business, change, and closure. The pain around death is mitigated by the faith to trust that everything is happening for the best and highest good for all concerned. We remain here in earthschool a while longer while the soul of our loved one embarks upon its journey through the afterlife, and all that that entails.

*   *   *

Fear is the most powerful negative human emotion. Fear of death is the ultimate fear. The common denominator to all phobias is the irrational terror that, if taken to an extreme, death would be the worst outcome. Until recently, death has been viewed as a mysterious unknown, eliciting images of a dreaded grim reaper. Some religions have instilled threats of hell and damnation if we are "bad", which further enhances anxieties about dying. From a social perspective, conjuring negative depictions surrounding transition has led to much trepidation associated with this very natural and irrevocable event. After all, none of us get out of this experience alive. Until recently, what we had to dissipate our apprehensions about death were the inspirational reassurances of ascended masters such as Moses, Jesus, Buddha, Krishna, and Mohammed. But these spiritual admonitions require faith. The kingdom of heaven is not tangible or visible.

For more than sixty years medical science has been using lifesaving machines to pull people from the jaws of death. With modern technology affording us numerous opportunities to fend off human demise, accounts of death experiences have supported the belief in an existence after this life that appeals to our rational mind. The scientist in all of us is reassured that this is not make-believe but real. Possibility evolves into probability and eventually into a knowing. As this process unfolds, fear is dispelled, replaced by the serenity that comes with acceptance.

Doctors often view death as a failure. It is the exceptional physician who does not emotionally withdraw from his or her patient when science can no longer forestall the inevitable. Without a spiritual framework to put death in perspective, fear predominates. The patient, family, and healthcare providers can form a conspiracy of doom and despair.

The loss of a loved one is often viewed as abandonment. The resultant fear can be oppressive. We want to blame ourselves or others. Lawyers take advantage of these feelings. A bad outcome becomes the basis for a lawsuit, and death is often perceived as the ultimate bad outcome.

It is the unknown that frightens us the most. As has been said,

> *What the caterpillar calls death*
> *The master calls a butterfly*

From the cocoon, from the shroud of death, emerges a beautiful creature light enough to fly. If we dwell on the darkness, unaware of our impending dance among the flowers, dread ensues. Fear grabs us in the pit of the stomach, overwhelming our faith with doubt and foreboding. It takes the master's wisdom and clarity to *see* past the opaque veil blocking the light, revealing a reality more expansive and comforting.

*　　*　　*

Hospice is a godsend.

The positivity of healing is witnessed most perfectly through the gentleness and dignity of assisting individuals through the dying process. Hospice is holistic in its approach to attending to the needs of those making the transition, and to all who surround those individuals. Hospice workers address not only the physical needs of comfort, cleanliness, and freedom from pain, but also the emotional difficulties people experience during this challenging time. Counseling is offered by trained professionals and, often profoundly, by unlicensed volunteers with a sympathetic ear and a kind heart. The spiritual needs of all concerned are an important focus. Done properly, this is individualized to the spiritual beliefs of the dying and their family—respect without proselytizing, and always with love.

As one candle may kindle many others and yet lose none of its own light, so we can share love and light with others and not be diminished in the process.

Many of the peak moments in my professional career have occurred at the bedside of an individual in transition surrounded by family and hospice workers. All who work with hospice are Light-workers. May God bless each and every one of you.

*   *   *

Euthanasia is a hotly debated issue among ethicists, healthcare givers, and clergy. Assisted suicide has received much media exposure from highly publicized events that have brought this subject into the light of public scrutiny. One point of view is that needless suffering from a terminal disease is cruel given medical science's ability to use medication to humanely end life. This is done to animals in good conscience every day. Why not extend that relief to human beings?

Those who feel life comes from God, and not within the realm of mere mortals to end at our discretion, argue that medicinal intervention goes against the natural order of life. Besides, humans are not animals. Although all life is sacred, human consciousness and animal consciousness are not the same. Human intellect and insight allow us to make some rational sense of the dying process, bringing a natural physical occurrence to a higher level of experience. What is merely prolonging the agony of an animal injured or dying, can be a valuable opportunity for spiritual growth for a human being. Whereas alleviating pain is the goal of humane medical therapy, the actual taking of a life may rob an individual of an invaluable chance for deathbed enlightenment.

The truth is that the medicines used to ease pain do, to some degree, facilitate death by their side-effect of suppressing the respiratory center in the brain. Since suffering is worse than death, society sanctions the use of therapeutic analgesics, in sufficient amounts to curtail pain, but short of lethal doses. This ethical compromise seems reasonable. Humane use of medication is warranted and morally acceptable, but taking it to the extreme of assisting in the demise of another human being becomes tantamount to murder, however it is justified. Euthanasia appears to cross an ethical line into realms of power that most of us feel uncomfortable wielding.

Seeing death from a spiritual perspective allows us to appreciate the magnificent possibilities for quantum leaps of soul growth during this natural process of transition. If fear is removed from the equation, death is no longer a dreaded event to be avoided at all costs, or hastened too quickly through human intervention. Dying can be allowed to take place unhindered, except to alleviate unnecessary pain.

Suicide at the end of life, not assisted by anyone else, is a separate issue. Taking one's own life is a matter between that person, their Higher self, and their Higher Power, and is no one else's business. Once another person is involved, however, a line is crossed. Whereas self-suicide is a matter of personal choice with karmic consequences, bringing another individual into the process makes assisted suicide a moral issue in our society.

Suicide is always an option for anyone, even in nonterminal situations. Most people shun that choice for several reasons: 1) fear that it is a mortal sin; 2) dread of self-inflicted pain; 3) lack of means or strength; 4) an inherent wisdom that it is not a preferred option, finding instead the courage to see life through to its proper conclusion. Of interest, those who have been interviewed after unsuccessful suicide attempts report their near-death experience as unpleasant. During their life review they regret their decision. Since we are here to endure life's pains and learn from our experiences, suicide is contrary to our overall purpose. Choosing suicide in one lifetime will make it more tempting in subsequent lives. Breaking the cycle in this incarnation will promote spiritual healing of this karmic issue.

Personally, I'm against the death penalty. Any person condemned to die should instead be placed in solitary confinement for the rest of their life. They would never leave their cell *for any reason* — complete isolation, given only food and water, and left alone to suffer until they die. Why? Death is a release — no more suffering. If society wants to punish people for committing horrific crimes, killing them only ends their suffering.

Death brings into focus the power and importance of the present moment. Although we may learn from the past, and plan for the future, being in the here and now is where we should be spending most of our time. We can't change the past, and the future is one big question mark. All we *really* have is the present moment. It is only in the here and now that we have any real power to change our lives.

* * *

A Buddhist or Hindu is raised understanding the concept of the karmic wheel of life, and readily accepts the birth-life-death-afterlife circle. Reincarnation is not part of the Judean, Christian, or Islamic philosophies and so meets with resistance among many.

Since rational science has been unable to prove, or disprove, rebirth, skepticism often prevails.

The cosmic transitioning from the Piscean to Aquarian age is facilitating a shift in human consciousness. New ideas are being introduced, and many old concepts are being reintroduced that heretofore were considered heresy or madness. Information is now available to every person who seeks it, made accessible through word of mouth, books, or via computer networking, that sheds new light on personal beliefs. True story accounts of death experiences, cross cultural and yet still hauntingly consistent, allow us to consider with more credibility the possibility of life after life. Regressive hypnosis permits a glimpse into previously unexplored realms of consciousness that also reinforce a circular pattern to our existence.

How and where souls originate is a human query unknowable to such limited beings as we Homo sapiens. If the soul is theoretically conceptualized as a spark of Divinity birthed from Source, having been created and liberated, it proceeds upon a path. The soul's inspiration for forward progression is growth. All living things grow. When they stop growing, they wither and die. Every existing entity seeks life-promoting energy for growth; the sun is the source of physical light, and Higher Power is the source of spiritual Light. The soul is instinctively motivated to pursue growth by its magnetic draw back to its origin. Born from Creation, it is released unto the experiences of being and growth, only to return full circle back from whence it came. Striving for perfection, the soul seeks physical form in order to have the life experiences necessary to provide the many opportunities to learn the lessons required for that individuated soul's advancement. Since we are all at different stages of soul development, we each have our own set of lessons we need to learn. Therefore, we have unique life stories, each individually tailored to our spiritual needs.

It is unrealistic to learn all essential lessons with only one try. How many times must a youngster attempt to tie his or her shoelaces before becoming proficient at that task? Humans learn from repetitive trial and error. It takes numerous attempts, and many failures, before success is achieved. Most people reach the end of their lives ideally having learned a few important lessons, but also leaving many other lessons only partially accomplished. Some issues seem like giant hurdles and others are not difficult to deal with at all. Whereas one may not be tempted to steal or cheat, learning patience may require many challenges, and yet still elude us by the time we die. Hence the need to reincarnate.

For any individual soul to achieve full actualization it requires many classes in earthschool. Becoming adept in all areas of human consciousness is the major undertaking of each of our souls. Numerous lifetimes are required. Death is therefore not an end to our existence, but rather a transition to the other side for respite and evaluation. Earthschool is difficult—we all deserve a summer vacation from pain and suffering. Since being human has its pleasurable moments, and because further education is required by the soul's fundamental desire for wholeness and perfection, rebirth occurs and class is back in session. Life review at the completion of any one incarnation serves as a springboard for determining the essential lessons to be addressed in the next life.

Karma is the driving force used to establish the array of lessons made available to any individual soul. Natural consequences for actions from a previous life formulate the framework for lessons to be learned in the next. For example, arrogance in one life will be balanced by defeat or indignity in the subsequent one. Karma has an infinite number of manifestations. Although the specific details vary from person to person, the basic lessons to be learned are common to us all. Eventually, every soul must experience, and come to terms with, the full range of human issues—in as many lifetimes as is required, one by one, until we find the correct balance for each. We must all experience, for example, anger and forgiveness, selfishness and generosity, and laziness and assertiveness, that we may find our spiritual center.

Karma is unfinished business. Opportunity lost in one life will be presented again and again in subsequent ones. It will be perceived as difficulty or pain, but essentially the underlying situation is designed to encourage the soul to finally triumph over any one particular human issue. This creation of an individually crafted lesson plan for each specific lifetime is karmically ordained by our Higher self. This is unconscious and not readily apparent to our logical mind, hence the appearance of fate beyond our control. In fact our soul desires growth, yearns for perfection, and is oblivious to physical pain. Our Higher self will karmically formulate a framework of events that will encompass challenges and difficulties devised to provide the setting to grasp incompletely mastered lessons, to practice whatever the archetypal issue is over and over again, until finally it becomes a nonissue.

Once we learn the lesson to our Higher self's satisfaction, the issue moves from foreground to background, making room for the next important lesson's focus of spiritual intention. Like peeling layers, one lesson learned reveals yet another, deeper level of needed growth to be addressed—one essential lesson after another, one lifetime after the other, until reincarnation into human form is no longer required. Graduation from earthschool occurs. What comes next transcends human understanding.

May your pains be small...
May your lessons be easy

Author's Note

The path of a teacher begins as a student. It requires a desire to learn, to seek answers and to be open to new ideas. I wish to acknowledge my important mentors to show my deep appreciation and respect.

The Beatles

Carlos Castaneda

Edgar Cayce

Chicago Medical School

Ram Dass

Wayne Dyer

Mahatma Gandhi

Jesus

Barry Kaufman

Patricia Millman

Rosalyn and Solomon Millman

Raymond Moody

Caroline Myss

Michael Newton

Tom Robbins

Eckhart Tolle

Machaelle Small Wright

Paramahansa Yogananda

Recommended Reading

Barbara Ann Brennan
  Hands of Light

Carlos Castaneda
  start with *The Teachings of Don Juan* and go from there

Gina Cerminara
  Many Mansions: The Edgar Cayce Story on Reincarnation

Ram Dass
  Be Here Now

Wayne W. Dyer, PhD
  You'll See It When You Believe It
  Real Magic
  Your Sacred Self
  Manifest Your Destiny
  Inspiration: Your Ultimate Calling

Masaru Emoto
  The Hidden Messages in Water

W. Y. Evans-Wentz
  The Tibetan Book of the Dead

Edith Fiore, PhD
  You Have Been Here Before
  The Unquiet Dead

Robert Fisher
The Knight in Rusty Armor

Thich Nhat Hanh
Being Peace

Tim Hansel
You Gotta Keep Dancin'

David Hawkins, MD, PhD
Power vs. Force

Louise L. Hay
You Can Heal Your Life

Esther and Jerry Hicks
Ask and It Is Given

Carl G. Jung, MD
Man and His Symbols

Barry Neil Kaufman
Happiness Is a Choice

Elisabeth Kubler-Ross, MD
On Death and Dying

Bruce Lipton, PhD
The Biology of Belief

Steven Locke, MD, and Douglas Colligan
The Healer Within: The New Medicine of Mind and Body

Raymond Moody, MD, PhD
Life After Life

Caroline Myss, PhD
Anatomy of the Spirit
Sacred Contracts

Michael Newton, PhD
Journey of Souls

M. Scott Peck, MD
The Road Less Traveled

Fritz Perls, MD
Gestalt Therapy Verbatim

Tom Robbins
start with *Another Roadside Attraction* and go from there

Sharon Salzberg
Lovingkindness

Eckhart Tolle
The Power of Now

Brian Weiss, MD
Many Lives, Many Masters

Marianne Williamson
A Return to Love

Machaelle Small Wright
Behaving as if the God in All Life Mattered

Paramahansa Yogananda
Autobiography of a Yogi

Gary Zukov
Seat of the Soul

CPSIA information can be obtained at www.ICGtesting.com
Printed in the USA
LVOW11s2317230214

374892LV00001B/79/P